CAPE MEARES
AND ITS SENTINEL

CLARA M. FAIRFIELD AND
M. WAYNE JENSEN, JR.

Published by
Tillamook County Pioneer Museum

Cover and back cover photographs:
Cape Meares Lighthouse
Carl Schonbrod, Tillamook, Oregon

Title page photograph:
A lovely summer day at Cape Meares, July 1961
Francis Seufert, The Dalles, Oregon

Page iv facing Table of Contents:
The beauty of the old lens is shown in this 1959 photograph.

Library of Congress Control Number: 00-135774
ISBN 0-9661150-1-5

For additional copies of this book, contact:
TILLAMOOK COUNTY PIONEER MUSEUM
2106 Second Street
Tillamook, OR 97141

Printed by Maverick Publications, Inc.
P.O. Box 5007 • Bend, OR 97708

Introduction

The Tillamook County Pioneer Museum was founded in 1935 by the Tillamook County Pioneer Association with a mission to preserve the rich heritage of the county. The old County Courthouse, built in 1905, became its home. When the burgeoning collection grew too large for the volunteer staff to handle, the Museum was deeded over to the County in 1945. In 1994 management was returned to the Pioneer Association. It is considered to be one of the finest small museums in the country.

M. Wayne Jensen, Jr., Director of the Museum, and Mrs. Clara M. Fairfield, curator, have collaborated on this book. The photos, letters, plans, artifacts, surveys and other public documents that Mr. Jensen has amassed and added to the Museum's collections over the last 25 years are the nucleus of this work.

Mrs. Fairfield wrote the text and designed the book and cover. Mr. Jensen provided the materials and answers to the obscure and often difficult questions that arose. The results should provide everything anyone would ever want to know about Cape Meares and its lighthouse—and then some.

But as is the case in anything involving history, new information is always coming to light. We will appreciate hearing from those who have information about the Keepers and their families and workmen who may have helped build or take down structures at the station. There are certain to be other stories involving the lighthouse we hope readers will share with us.

We know there are many pictures hiding in old family albums. Please let us make copies of them to add to the Museum's wonderful collection of Tillamook County's only lighthouse. The proceeds realized from this publication benefit the Tillamook County Pioneer Museum.

TABLE OF CONTENTS

1899 photograph of Cape Meares by E. Meresse

Geological Beginnings

The beauty of the North Oregon coast is a product of its geologic past. Sixty million years ago, during the Eocene Epoch, vast amounts of lava erupted from vents on the sea floor. This activity stretched from Vancouver Island south to the Klamath Mountains. In the northern part of the Coast Range these rocks are known as the Tillamook Volcanic Series. They continued to accumulate over a long period of time until in some places they were 20,000 feet thick and had formed large volcanic islands. In the mountains north and east of Tillamook, outcroppings of these rocks are visible. Pillow lavas, formed when lava was extruded under water, can be seen just west of the summit on State Highway 6.

A large land mass rose above sea level east of Tillamook thirty five million years ago during Oligocene time. The sediments eroded from the uplifted rocks were deposited on the sea floor to the west and contain many marine fossils that can now be seen in hills north and south of Tillamook.

Twenty-five million years ago in the early Miocene Epoch, the Coast Range was elevated and the older rocks were folded and faulted. All but the western margin of Oregon was above sea level where local downwarpings formed shallow marine embayments. The Tillamook area is one of these basins. There are others in the Astoria, Newport and Coos Bay regions. Sediments from these uplifted lands filled the bays along with more marine specimens. These silt and sandstone deposits are called the Astoria Formation and were named for the location where they were first described. Outcroppings of this formation along the south side of Tillamook Bay near the oyster plant, and on the south side of Cape Lookout in the road cuts, produce many marine fossils.

Basalt was being extruded onto the sea floor at the same time the Astoria Formation sediments were being deposited. These outpourings of lava were the same as those being extruded over vast areas of the Pacific Northwest. From eastern Washington, western Idaho and north central Oregon west to the Coast Range, enormous amounts of lava flowed from vents all over the region in many succeeding flows. These flows were first described in the Columbia River Gorge and are known throughout their range as Columbia River Basalts. In the Tillamook area two centers of this volcanic activity were Cape Meares and Cape Lookout.

The center of the flow downwarped between the two Capes in the Netarts Bay area. The south edge of Cape Lookout is very high and dips to the north while Cape Meares is high on the north and dips to the south. Maxwell Mountain and the Three Arched Rocks are part of the Cape Meares flow. Both Capes show a predominate 10° dip to the west. Pillow lavas can be found at the base of both Capes and magnificent columnar-jointed basalts may be seen on

Basalt columns on the south side of Cape Lookout are 100 feet high, and stretch over a half-mile in length.

the south side of Cape Lookout where they stand over a hundred feet high and a half-mile long.

These basalts form most of the spectacular headlands and off-shore rocks on the northern Oregon coast. Cape Meares, and its neighbor to the south, were both candidates for a lighthouse.

The Wildlife

There are more than 50 species of mammals in the area including elk, deer, bear, cougar, coyote, beaver, river otter, bobcat, raccoon, mink, muskrat, rabbits, squirrels, mice, voles, and shrews. Wolves are now extinct and opossums were introduced about 70 years ago. There are resident colonies of seals and sea lions. Sea otters are extinct and gray whales are migrant visitors. Orcas are frequently seen. At least 240 species of birds have been recorded. There are over 60 species of fish inhabiting the rivers, bays and coastal waters. Tillamook Bay has one of the finest salmon fisheries in the world.

Steller Sea Lion (Eumetopias Jubata), top left; Common Murres (Uria Aalge), bottom left; and the Tufted Puffin (Lunda Currgata), above.

3

First Inhabitants

Salish speaking people from the Northwest Coast settled this coastal strip about 500 years ago. The name Tillamook, a Chinook word, refers to the people that lived near the mouth of the rivers and along the shores of the bays. They were further divided into villages and family groups known as Nehalem, Netarts, Nestucca, Salmon River and Siletz.

Chief Illga Adams, circa 1850s

Tillamook Head, near Seaside, was their northern boundary with the largest concentration centered around the five rivers that flow into Tillamook Bay. The southern boundary was near Otter Rock, south of Siletz Bay. Their culture centered around cedar and salmon. The cedar provided them with the material to make their plank houses, clothing, baskets and dugout canoes. Canoes were their principal means of transportation.

Always abundant, salmon was their main food staple. There was so much, that by smoking and drying, they had a year-round food supply with extra for trading. Another food staple was dried shellfish. Mounds of shells can still be seen at Cape Lookout and on the Netarts sand spit where they harvested clams from the bay and mussels from the rocks at the base of both capes.

Maggie Adams, wife of Illga Adams

Maggie Adams and Lizzie, daughter of Maggie and Illga, circa 1880s.

Traces of their well-worn trails over these headlands are still visible. They traded many miles beyond their home territory in their ocean-going canoes—up and down the coast and as far east as The Dalles on the Columbia River. They were able to peacefully co-exist with their non-Salish speaking neighbors by means of trade and intermarriage.

Early Explorers

John Meares (1756-1809)

John Meares entered the British Royal Navy in 1771 with the rating of "Captain's Servant" and passed his examination on September 17, 1778 when he was 22 years old. The next day he was promoted to the rank of Lieutenant. In 1783 he joined the merchant fleet and sailed to India. There he helped organize the first European trading expedition to the northwest coast of America on the ship *Nootka* in 1786. They were looking for the furs reported by famed English explorer Captain James Cook in 1778.

It seems Meares was somewhat of a scoundrel—his exploitation of the natives led to a lot of trouble for those that came after him. He made several trips to the northwest coast and wrote an exciting account of them. There was heated controversy over their accuracy at the time. Little was heard of Meares again until his promotion to Commander on February 26, 1795. He died in 1809.

Captain John Meares was the first Englishman to chart the northernmost of the two capes on July 6, 1788. He named it Cape Lookout. The bay just to the north he dubbed Quick Sand Bay.

In August of the same year, Captain Robert Gray, the first American on the west coast of North America, sailed his ship the *Lady Washington* into the same bay on August 14, 1788. Gray did not mention the cape, but named the bay Murderer's Harbor. This was because of the loss of a cabin boy to the local Indians while the ship was anchored there replenishing water and fresh food and trading for furs. The Bay is now called Tillamook, named for the natives that inhabited the area.

Lieutenant John Meares, British Navy officer, was the first to describe the Cape on July 6, 1788.

The Settlers Come

Contact with outsiders and their communicable diseases drastically reduced the native population. When Joe Champion arrived by whaleboat from Astoria on April 2, 1851, there were only a few hundred Tillamooks left. Meriwether Lewis had estimated their number to be over 2,000 in 1806.

The geographically isolated area could only be reached by ship over shallow bars or by the few trails over the mountains north, south and east. The *Morning Star,* built in Tillamook, was launched on

Joseph Champion, a bachelor and Tillamook's first white settler (above) and his "Castle" of a hollow spruce tree (left) as produced in replica in the Tillamook Pioneer Museum.

January 5, 1855. It was the first of many ships built in the county. The Trask River toll road to Yamhill was the first road into the county and was opened in 1872.

The First Lights

Alexandria

For untold centuries, a bonfire on a hill was all an ancient mariner could expect to guide him to his home port at night. The Egyptians spent 20 years building a tower on the island of Pharos that rose 450 feet high. It soared above the Nile River delta at Alexandria in 300 B.C. The light was an open fire built at the top of the magnificent structure.

The lighthouse was lit for about 1,000 years. The unused tower remained for another 600 years before it was destroyed by an earthquake in 1349. Archaeological examination indicates the base was 400 feet on each side and was probably a fortification for the protection of the harbor. The tower was built in at least two tiers and covered with white marble.

The Romans began building lighthouses around their empire at least 50 years before the birth of Christ. The 100 foot structure at Ostia (the mouth of the Tiber River, Rome's port) was the first. At least 30 more lighthouse sites have been identified as having been built by them before their decline in the fifth century. The Romans were probably the ones who built a lighthouse at Corunna on the northwest coast of Spain some time before the fourth century.

Records indicate the tower was a square stone structure 130 feet tall. A legend says that Hercules built the tower and placed the fire on it that burned for 300 years. Ships bound for England used its beacon. After the light went out, the Spanish government restored the pillar by encasing it in a tower of granite.

The light still functions today and as far as is known, it is the world's oldest lighthouse.

At the end of the Dark Ages, about 1100 A.D., trade between the

Pharos of Alexandria from an old engraving.

European countries increased and lighthouses were needed to facilitate shipping. Water was the principle means of travel and lights began to appear along rivers and seacoasts. Estimates indicate that there were 34 lighthouses along the European coast line by 1600. Construction continued and by 1800 there were 175.

Wesc Coasc Lighcs

The first lighthouse on the west coast of America was erected by Cortez at the harbor of Salina Cruz, New Spain (Mexico) in the 1550s. Built of adobe, the square structure had a brazier on the top to hold the open fire.

A lighthouse was incorporated into the design of Alexander Baranoff's castle at Sitka, the capitol of Russian Alaska in 1837. Consisting of four small cups of seal oil with wicks backed by a reflector, they were housed in the cupola of the building 100 feet above the sea. This welcomed sentinel was the first in the Pacific Northwest and far superior to the bonfires and ship's lanterns that had been used before it was lit.

Baranoff's Castle at Sitka, Alaska, circa 1894.

Colonial Lights

The Boston Light on Little Brewster Island in Boston Harbor was the earliest lighthouse built in the Colonies. It was lit for the first time on September 14, 1716. Although the British blew up the structure in 1776 during the Revolutionary War, it was rebuilt in 1783. A cannon, the first known fog signal, had been placed at the station in 1719.

The Sandy Hook lighthouse on the New Jersey side of the entrance to New York Harbor was built in 1764. This is the oldest U.S. lighthouse still in use.

The Boston light tower on Little Brewster Island in Boston Harbor is 89 feet high and now houses a first-order lens.

The Sandy Hook Lighthouse is an octagonal stone tower 85 feet high. Its builder was Issac Conro and it was financed by lottery funds in 1765.

Brief History of the Lighthouse Service

One of the first bills passed by the new Federal Government of the United States was to establish a lighthouse system. It would be responsible for all aids to navigation and took over all existing lighthouses, including four that were under construction. This was the first public works act and was signed by President George Washington on August 7, 1789. The Secretary of the Treasury would be the administrator.

Fifth Auditor of the Treasury, Stephen Pleasonton

George Washington (Reproduced from the *Dictionary of American Portraits,* published by Dover Publications, Inc. in 1967, painting by Gilbert Stuart.)

Prior to this the individual colonies were responsible for their own aids to navigation. By 1792 the lighthouses had been assigned to the Commissioner of Revenue and part of the keepers' duties were to collect customs. In 1802 the Secretary of the Treasury resumed control until 1813 when they were returned to the Commissioner of Revenue. In 1820 the aids to navigation became the responsibility of the Fifth Auditor of the Treasury. This man's name was Stephen Pleasonton. By

1842 there were 256 lighthouses, 30 floating lights plus 35 beacons and nearly 1,000 buoys.

Mr. Pleasonton, who was known as the Superintendent of Lighthouses, ran a very frugal department. He handled all personnel matters—hiring, firing, and paying keepers—authorized purchases of land and selection of sites, repairs and all legitimate expenditures. His economy led to ineffectiveness and deterioration. After many reports of navigation troubles, Congress ordered the "Inspection of 1838."

As a result, six Atlantic Coast and two Great Lakes districts were formed with an experienced naval officer assigned to each one. This helped some, but matters continued to deteriorate. An example: the Fresnel (fra-nell) lens that had been developed in 1822 and was used by nearly all European countries with vastly improved results was rejected by Pleasonton because he thought they cost too much. In 1838, he was ordered to purchase two, one first-order fixed lens and one second-order revolving lens. They were installed at Navesink, New Jersey, Light Station in 1849. He insisted on retaining the old lamp and reflector system for the other lights.

The keepers were often political appointments and had little training and were poorly paid. They were expected to hold down other jobs to supplement their income. There were more abuses—lightships having to leave posts to pick up supplies because of the lack of tenders—lights with short visibility that were poorly maintained and not sited in the right place. The U.S. Lighthouse Service was now the worst in the civilized world.

Complaints built to a point where Congress again had to take action. In 1847 construction of six lighthouses was transferred to the Army Corps of Engineers and in 1851 Congress took another step to solve the troubles. The Congress required the Secretary of the Treasury to convene a board composed of two high-ranking naval officers, two army engineers, a civilian of high scientific attainment, and a junior officer of the Navy to act as secretary of the board. This inspection of the Lighthouse Service led to a report of 760 pages with many illustrations. They recommended a complete revamping of the system following the examples of England, Scotland, Ireland, and France, which were well known for their fine navigational aids.

Congress, with little urging, accepted the Board's recommendations and on October 9, 1852, created the nine-member Lighthouse Board under the Treasury Department. This establishment was divided into 16 districts. Each was directed by an inspector and an engineer, the former being Navy and the latter Army officers. The Board had supervision of all administrative duties relating to the construction and maintenance of lighthouses, light-vessels, beacons, fog-signals, buoys, and their appendages, and had charge of all records and property appertaining to the establishment. They went to work immediately on this massive job.

All kinds of reforms and improvements were made; Fresnel lenses replaced all old lamps. Some towers were raised for better visibility. More lighthouse tenders were added and replacement ships were available for any lightships that were storm damaged or in need of major maintenance. They sought out good keepers and trained them to their tasks. The keepers' duties were completely spelled out in manuals and the Board did not hesitate to fire those who would not maintain a good light. Adequate spare parts were kept at each station and if major repairs were needed, engineers in each district were available to take care of them. The primary concern of the Board was that there would always be a light where the mariner expected to find it.

Aids to navigation in the United States improved rapidly and the reputation of the Lighthouse Service went from the worst to the best. The United States soon led the world in developing and using new techniques and has ever since.

As the service grew, the nine-member Lighthouse Board found it difficult to manage such a large system effectively. By 1910 there were 11,713 aids to navigation of all types in 16 districts. Friction occurred between the Naval officers in charge of navigational aids and the Army Corps of Engineers in charge of new construction and repairs. Congress passed an act on June 17, 1910 to abolish the old Lighthouse Board and establish, under one head, the Bureau of Lighthouses governed by the Department of Commerce.

The military discipline of the old Lighthouse Board was in good part responsible for the vast improvements in the system. The transfer of the new Bureau to civilian management eased the tensions and reduced costs.

The man selected to be commissioner was George R. Putnam. He entered the service of the U.S. Coast and Geodetic Survey after graduating as an engineer and served with them for the next 20 years. During his tenure, the U.S. Lighthouse Service became the largest such organization in the world. The number of districts increased to 19, now including Alaska, Puerto Rico and the Hawaiian Islands. By 1924, it had 16,888 aids to navigation and more automatic equipment than any other country. The introduction of radio beacons, electric buoys and electric fog signals was achieved. The number of aids had doubled and at the same time the number of employees had decreased by 20 percent. Putnam retired in 1935.

Four years later, under the Presidential Reorganization Act of 1939, the Bureau of Lighthouses was abolished and all personnel and equipment moved from the jurisdiction of the Commerce Department to that of the United States Coast Guard.

The Bill provided for the induction of Lighthouse personnel into the Coast Guard without loss of rank or any reduction in annual compensation. Credit would be received for service already completed relating to retirement benefits.

This progressive outlook, starting with the Lighthouse Board, has continued through the years and the Coast Guard has kept up with the latest improvements in aids to navigation. Introduction of Loran (Long-Range Navigation) and Shoran (Short-Range Navigation) systems at appropriate Coast Guard stations has made the navigators' job much easier. They can now receive these strong radio signals and determine the exact position of their ships. This is an additional safety factor for it allows the ship to remain farther off shore in deeper water. Automated equipment has allowed the placing of lights and radio signals where manned stations would be impossible to maintain. The Lighthouse Service has come a long way from a peak of 800 lighthouses at the turn of the century. About 500 remain, and of those, only 32 are manned. The Coast Guard has completed automation of all its lighthouses.

Pacific Coast to get Lighthouses

The object of lighthouse placement in lighting a coastline was to set towers so their beams of light would meet and pass each other. With such an arrangement, a ship would never be out of sight of a light.

necessary. In the order of construction these were:

Umpqua	1857–1861
Cape Arago	1866
Cape Blanco	1870
Yaquina Bay	1871
Yaquina Head	1873
Point Adams	1875
Tillamook Rock	1881
Cape Meares	1890
Heceta Head	1892
Columbia River	
Lightship	1892
Umpqua River	1894
Coquille River	1895

Zachary Taylor was the twelfth President of the United States, serving from 1849 until he died in office in 1850.

After Congress ratified an 1848 bill to erect lighthouses on the west coast, President Zachary Taylor authorized a Pacific Coast Survey party in 1849. The survey was to select sites for two lighthouses and two buoys on the Oregon coast. The surveyors were then to proceed along the California coastline and find additional sites suitable for lighthouses. All sites were to be selected from public lands.

Cape Disappointment was the first location to be selected. This was in 1849 but the project was not completed until 1856. The mouth of the Umpqua River was next. A lighthouse there was finished in 1857. Cape Disappointment, at the north entrance to the Columbia River, is now in the state of Washington, but this was Oregon Territory when it was built. The first U.S. lighthouse completed on the Pacific coast was built on Alcatraz Island in San Francisco Bay in 1854.

As ship traffic increased along the Oregon coast, more lighthouses were

The Honorable John H. Mitchell of Oregon served four terms in the U.S. Senate: 1873, 1885, 1801, and 1901.

SENATE APPROPRIATIONS INTRODUCED

By 1885, an additional lighthouse between Yaquina Head and Tillamook Rock was needed to fill the dangerous 84 mile gap. The Honorable John H. Mitchell, U.S. Senator from Oregon, introduced Senate Bill 1216 on January 25, 1886. The long involved building process began.

49TH CONGRESS, 1ST SESSION

S. 1216.

IN THE SENATE OF THE UNITED STATES.

JANUARY 25, 1886.

Mr. MITCHELL, of Oregon, introduced the following bill; which was read twice and referred to the Committee on Commerce.

A BILL

Making an appropriation for the purchase of a site and the construction of a light-house at Cape Meares, Tillamook Bay, Oregon.

1   *Be it enacted by the Senate and House of Representa-*

2   *tives of the United States of America in Congress assembled,*

3   That the sum of sixty thousand dollars be, and the same is

4   hereby, appropriated, out of any moneys in the Treasury not

5   otherwise appropriated, for the purchase of a site and the

6   construction of a first-order coast light-house at Cape Meares,

7   Tillamook Bay, Oregon.

49TH CONGRESS,
1ST SESSION.

H. R. 5862.

IN THE HOUSE OF REPRESENTATIVES.

JUNE 9, 1886.

Referred to the Committee on Commerce with the amendments of the Senate and ordered to be printed.

Insert the part printed in *italics*.

AN ACT

Providing for the establishment of a light-house and fog-signal at San Luis Obispo, California.

H.R. 5862, with amendments from the Senate, was referred to the Committee on Commerce and ordered to be printed on June 9, 1886. Lines in the amendment affecting Oregon were:

51   *shall not exceed the sum of fifteen thousand dollars; also*

52   *for the purchase of a site and the construction of a first-order*

53   *coast light-house at Cape Meares, Tillamook Bay, Oregon,*

54   *the cost of which shall not exceed the sum of sixty thousand*

55   *dollars; also that the appropriation of fifteen thousand dol-*

56   *lars made by the act of Congress approved July seventh,*

57   *eighteen hundred and eighty-four, "for removing the Croatan*

Letters from the Lighthouse Board

Excerpts from correspondence indexes, pertaining to the building and operation of the Cape Meares Light Station, give an accurate chronology of the events that happened. Letters will be cited from time to time to emphasize certain points.

The Tillamook County Pioneer Museum obtained copies of the letter indexes, the earliest dated December 20, 1886. The indexes give dates, name of writer, address (where the letter was sent) and the subject of the correspondence. The bound Letter Book number and page number were included, but unfortunatley, the Letter Books have not been located. With these historical files, one truly has the opportunity to read between the lines.

(No. 1.)

WRITER.	ADDRESS.	DATE.

C. & G. Survey ___ Washington, D.C. ___ 20 Dec. 1886

Subject: Cape Meares and Cape Lookout - Oreg. - Tracings of headlands - and letter rel. to L.H. site - transmitted.

Bound in Letter Book No. 716 ......, Page 910 , with ...3 enclosures.

Surveys Begin

The first survey undertaken to establish a site was arranged by Captain Charles F. Powell, U.S. Army Corps of Engineers. His instructions to J.S. Polhemus were to examine both Cape Meares and Cape Lookout. That information would then be used to select a site for a lighthouse.

The original of the following report was handwritten:

L.H. 40

Report on an Examination
of
Cape Meares and Cape Lookout

Oregon

with referene to the selection of a

Light House site
made in May, 1886
by
J.S. Polhemus.

Extract & originale of maps
for'd to L.H. Board Feb. 14th

U.S. Engineer Office
Portland, Oregon

June 2, 1886
Captain Charles F. Powell
Corps of Engineers, U.S.A.

Sir:

In accordance with your verbal instructions of May 18th. I have proceeded to make an examination of Cape Meares and Cape Lookout on the Oregon Coast, with reference to the selection of a site for a Light House.

I went from here to Astoria and proceeded thence by sea in the steam schooner *Rosie Olsen* to Tillamook Bay some 47 miles south of the mouth of the Columbia River. After landing on the north shore of the Bay I crossed over in a small boat to the extreme Southern shore a distance of about 4 miles, and about one mile along the beach to the commencement of the Cape Meares. The extreme point of which is reached by a trail about one mile long leading from the beach back up through the timber and brush.

I spent parts of two days on Cape Meares and made a sketch by eye which accompanies this report. I also measured the elevation of the seaward extremity of the bluff with a marked cord and took compass bearings to the principle headlands visible, north and south.

Cape Meares is a rocky headland on the Oregon coast in Lat. 45° - 25' North and Longitude 123° - 57' West from Greenwich.

It is formed by the termination of a heavily timbered ridge about 1,000 feet high lying on the south side of Tillamook Bay.

It slopes gradually from its summit and projects a little over 1/2 a mile into the sea ending in precipitous cliffs of basalt from 200 to 400 feet in height.

It is situated 27 miles south of Tillamook Rock Light House, and 40 miles north of Foulweather Light House; and between the Headlands of the False Tillamook on the north and Cape Lookout on the south.

From the entrance of Tillamook Bay, a broad smooth sand beach, backed by a low ridge of Sand dunes, extends for about 4 miles to the north face of the Cape. From which point it juts into the ocean about 1/2 a mile.

Its general width between beaches is one mile. A trail leads up over the Cape at an elevation of about 800 feet, down to a short beach of about 3/4 of a mile, and then over a rocky point, called the Bald Mountain, to the north shore of Netarts Bay, a shallow sandy lagoon about 5 miles long, which is really all sand flats at low water. In this bay is a natural oyster bed. I am informed there is a depth on the Netarts Bar of 5 to 6 feet at mean low tide, and small vessels used to come in after oysters several years ago. There is very little agriculture or grazing land on the shores of this bay, which are very sparsely inhabited.

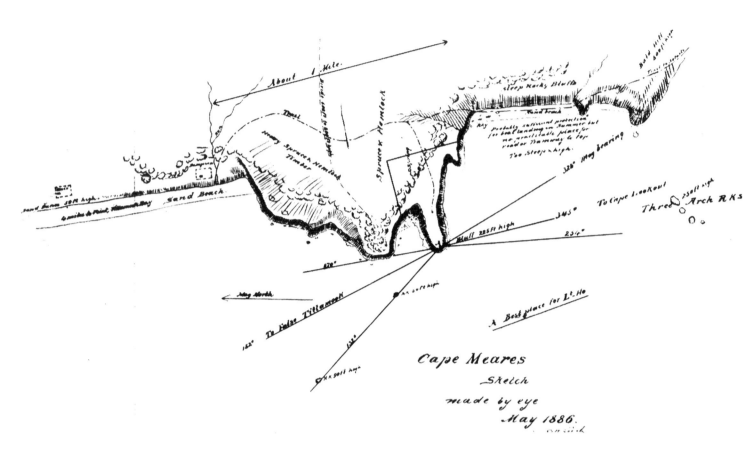

Cape Meares
Sketch
made by eye
May 1886.

The top of Cape Meares is covered with a good soil supporting over the greater part a thick growth of Spruce and Hemlock timber; at its extreme end it divides into two small rocky points about 800 to 1,000 feet apart. The southern most one is the most suitable site for a light house, extending two or three hundred feet farther into the sea, and being over 100 feet lower on top of the bluff and free from timber.

It is a small projecting ridge from three to four hundred feet wide on top, extending about 800 feet into the sea, with basaltic bluffs at the end 225 feet high.

It is covered with soil on which is growing, salmonberry, salal, fern, and wild grass. At the extreme end it is a good site for a light house with an elevation above the sea of 225 feet; back of this the ground gradually rises from 10 to 20 feet in a hundred.

The North point of the Cape is considerably higher and timbered, but does not extend out far enough to shut out the view of the coast North of Tillamook Bay.

From the southern point of the Cape the shore trends easterly in a bold basaltic cliff from 250 to 400 feet high, for about 1/2 a mile, terminating in a high rocky bluff in front of which a beach of gravel and sand extends for over half a mile to the south. This beach is sheltered in the summer time during the prevalence of N.W. winds and would probably afford a moderately good landing at smooth times, but the rocky bluffs surrounding it are so high and precipitous that there is no practicable chance for a road or tramway to be built leading to the top of the Cape.

On top of Cape Meares, just in the edge of the timber, about 1,000 feet from the point, and about 150 feet higher, is a small flowing spring, which would furnish all the water needed for construction purposes.

The basaltic rock crops out on the top of the Cape and by a little uncovering would afford broken stone for concrete.

Viewed from sea Cape Meares, although not quite so prominent as Cape Lookout, is still a conspicuous Headland.

To the South between 1 and 2 miles and less than a mile from the shore lies a group of four rocks; the outer one is not high; the three inner ones are larger and from 150 to 250 feet in height, and are remarkable in being perforated by tunnels or arches. They are called the "Three Arch Rocks".

The largest one is about 300 square feet sloping to a ridge on top. They would not interfere with the visibility of a light 50 feet high on Cape Meares.

A small rock about 60 feet square and 60 feet high lies immediately in front of the Cape; and a larger rock about 1 mile to the N.W. about 100 feet in height.

From the point of Cape Meares the Magnetic bearing to Cape Lookout is S. 15° E. The Mag. bearing to False Tillamook is N. 28° W.

To construct a Light House on Cape Meares, a wagon road would have to be built from the beach near Sampson's place on the north side of the Cape to its end.

It would not exceed two miles in length, with a summit about 600 feet or 700 feet high, and would cost for a good road about $500 per mile.

There is no beach or convenient landing place on the Cape where construction material could be landed. It would have to be brought over Tillamook Bay into the Bay in vessels drawing at the most 14 ft. and landed on the south shore of the Bay, either by building a small wharf, to cost about $500, or in lighters. The material would then have to be hauled from 1 to 2 miles on the beach, and about 2 miles more on the graded road to be built, to the point of the Cape.

There is about 14 or 15 feet depth on Tillamook Bar at mean-lower-low-tide and the channel is straight and well marked.

Inside the bay are many broad sand and mud flats, but a small channel runs from the entrance along the south shore inside for a mile or two.

There is a saw-mill on the Bay at which good fir and spruce lumber can be obtained for $10.00 per thousand.

Cut stone, brick, lime etc. would have to be shipped to the bay. Sand and gravel would have to be hauled from the beach.

The township lines of the U.S. Land Survey have not been extended quite to the extremity of Cape Meares; and the portion of land required for a Light House Reservation cannot be designated by Land Office section, or lot.

I have laid off a piece on sketch between the blue lines and the ocean, inclosing 60 or 80 acres, taking in the open land, spring of water, and some timber; which it would be desirable to have reserved for Light House purposes.

This land as well as that in the immediate neighborhood is unsettled and not desirable for agricultural purposes.

EXAMINATION OF CAPE LOOKOUT

From Tillamook Bay I traveled on foot by the trail over Cape Meares to Netarts Bay, crossed this bay in a small boat and proceeded down the sand beach six miles to Cape Lookout, climbed up the trail leading to the dividing ridge of the Cape, a distance of about 1 3/4 miles from the beach at the north side of the Cape. The ridge at this place has an altitude of about 900 feet.

From this point no trail leads to the end of the Cape, and I had to make my way as best I could on foot through thick brush and over and under fallen timber a distance of over two miles following most of the time bear trails.

I took two men with me as guides and helpers and consumed a day in getting out to the point and back.

After completing this examination I went by boat and trail to Tillamook Landing on a slough at the head of the bay, and by buckboard to the railroad station at North Yamhill and thence to Portland.

Cape Lookout is one of the most prominent headlands on the coast; it is situated at Lat. 45° - 14' N., Longitude 123° - 58 1/2' West eleven miles south of Cape M.

It is the termination of a heavily timbered ridge with an elevation at its highest point of about 2,500 feet; sloping gradually to its end, where it falls off by precipitous cliffs of basalt 400 or 500 feet high into the ocean. It is about 1 3/4 miles wide between beaches, at which place it is about 900 feet high.

It extends sharply into the sea about 2 miles, crossed by 2 or 3 ravines from 200 to 300 feet deep.

The dividing ridge is near the South side. The land falls away from it on this side in very steep slopes covered with slight herbage ending in rocky precipices three to five hundred feet high.

To the North of the divide the Cape is heavily timbered with Spruce and Hemlock to the rocky cliffs 300 to 400 feet high.

The ocean face of the cape is about 1,200 feet across and presents a steep bluff of basalt about 400 feet high. I was not able to get down to the water and can only estimate the distance.

There is no room to build a Light House on this Cape lower than 350 feet.

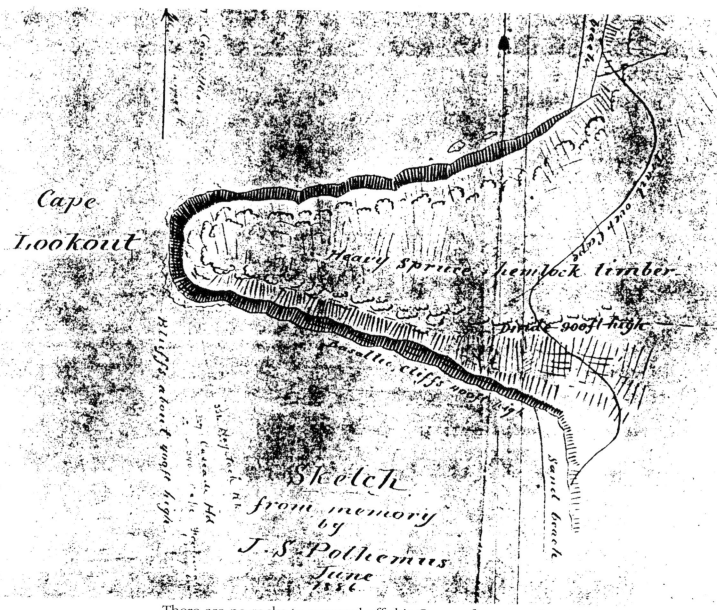

There are no rocks to seaward off this Cape, a few rugged rocks appear on the North side close in shore.

About nine miles to the south and 1 mile or less from the shore Haystack Rock rises out of the sea to a height of about 350 feet.

From Cape Lookout to opposite this rock and beyond a smooth sand beach extends.

Near this rock the Nestucca River empties into the ocean; about 10 feet of water can be found over its bar at high-tide.

The first Cape to the South of Lookout is Cascade Head about twenty miles away.

Cape Lookout presents a very salient point for the Light House, and it more nearly divides the distance between the Light Houses on Tillamook Rock and at Cape Foulweather, but from the nature of the ground a Light House would have to be higher than is desirable, and the difficulties to be encountered in getting materials of construction in place would be great.

No fresh water was seen in the neighborhood of the point although no doubt it can be found towards the bottoms of some of the small ravines.

Cape Lookout projects so far & so abruptly into the sea that it affords good protection on the south side for boat landing during the north west weather of summer.

But even if material was landed on either side of the Cape it would be almost impracticable to get it to the top of the Cape by a wagon road or tramway.

If a light was built on this Cape, I think a sheltered place on the south side near the end will have to be equipped with a large overhanging derrick, and material hoisted up from vessels by it, over the bluff and transported to the top by a tramway.

A good deal of difficulty will be experienced in getting material into place.

Cape Meares only ten or eleven miles to the north affords nearly as good a site as far as the view from the sea is concerned, and being lower gives a better situation of light with reference to fogs; and besides would be much easier of construction on account of its accessibility from Tillamook Bay.

A rough sketch from memory of Cape Lookout accompanies this report. The land is wild and unsettled and unsurveyed.

If the land survey lines were extended over Cape Lookout it would be in T. 1S., R. 11W. Willamette Meridian; and the extremity of Cape Meares would be in T. 3S., R.11W. Willamette Meridian.

> Very Respectively
> Your Obedient Servant,
> J.S. Polhemus

Note: The Township figures in the Polhemus report are printed as he wrote them. It is believed he inadvertently switched the two localities. Cape Meares is T.1 S., R.11 W. and Cape Lookout is T.3 S., R.11 W

Date: 12/20/1886

To: Washington, D.C.

From: Coast and Geodetic Survey

Subject: Cape Meares and Cape Lookout, Oregon. Tracings of Headlands & letters relating to L.H. site transmitted

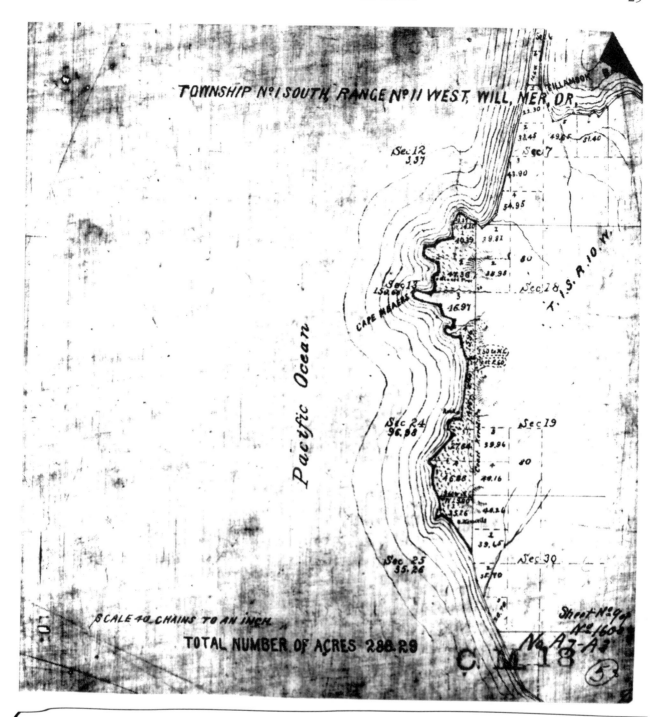

Date: 1/22/1887

To: Washington, D.C.

From: Hon. John H. Mitchell

Subject: Cape Meares, Oregon. Purchase of site. Appropriation
made. Information asked.

Date: 3/5/1887

To: Lighthouse Board

From: Location committee

Subject: Cape Meares, Oregon. Light Station establishment
recommended.

Date: 4/29/1887

To: Treasury Department

From: Secretary of Treasury

Subject: Cape Meares & other lands in Oregon. Withdraw from
sale – Lighthouse Reserve proposed.

Date: 6/1/1887

To: 13th District

From: Engineer C.F. Powell

Subject: Cape Meares, Ore. Plans & tracings of proposed buildings
– forward with recommendations

Date: 6/15/1887

To: 13th District

From: Engineer C. F. Powell

Subject: Cape Meares, Ore. Plans for proposed barn forwarded.

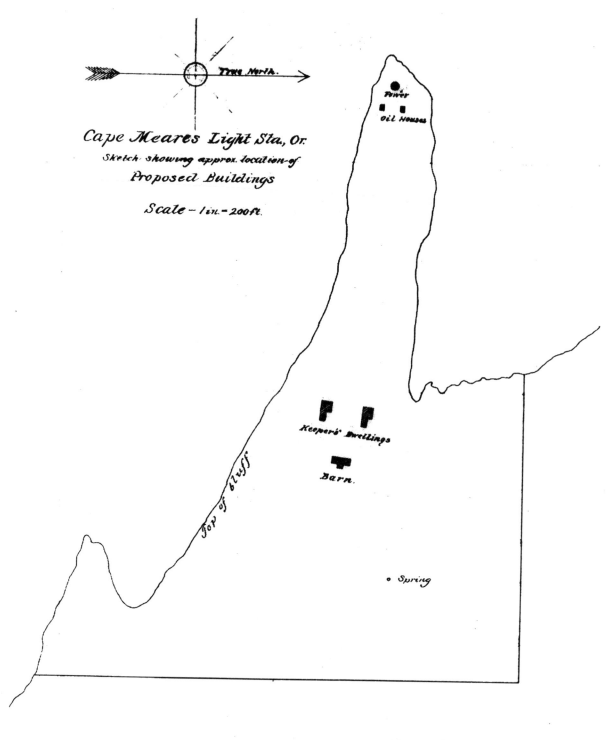

Sketch showing approximate location of proposed buildings for Cape Meares Light Station, Oregon, May 1887.

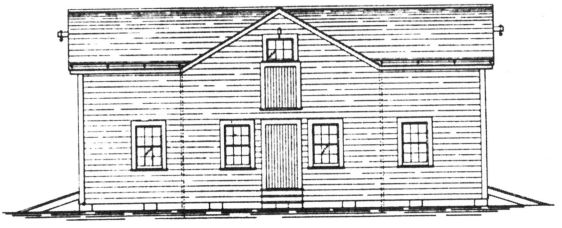

Front Elevation

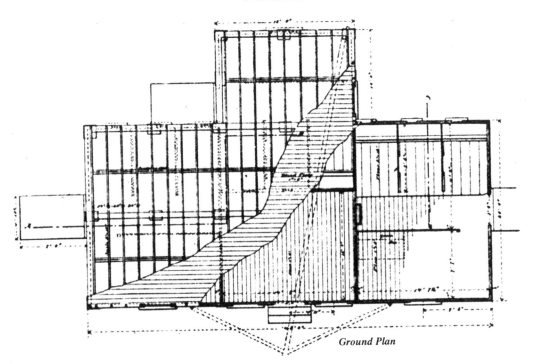

Ground Plan

Plans for barn, June 15, 1887.

Date: 6/29/1887

To: Lighthouse Board

From: Engineering Committee

Subject: Cape Meares, Ore. Structure - plans with recommendations
submitted.

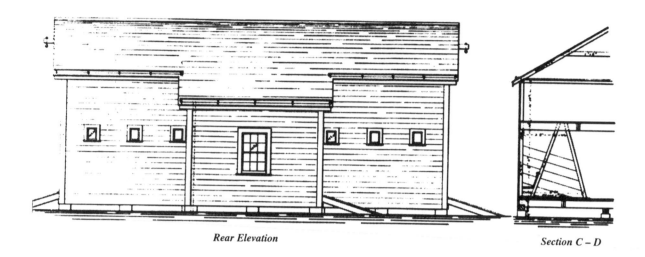

Rear Elevation

Section C – D

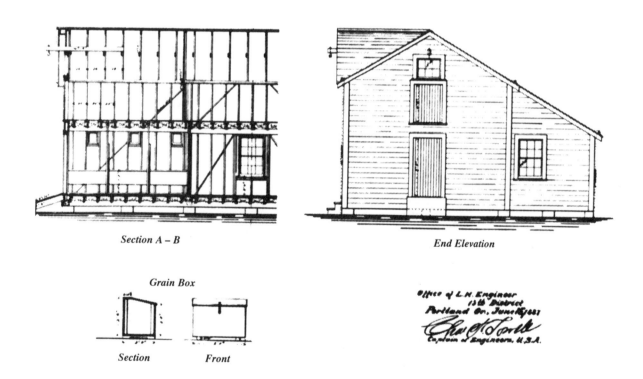

Section A – B

End Elevation

Grain Box

Section

Front

Plans for barn, June 15, 1887.

Side Elevation

Rear Elevation

Front Elevation

Office of L. H. Engineer, 13th Dist.
Portland, Or. May 1887
Chas F. Powell
Captain of Engineers U.S.A.
L. H. Engineer

Scale

Plans for the principal Keeper's dwelling, May 1887. Wording in box: The principal Keeper's dwelling is to be as here shown, except that the box stairs are to be omitted, and doors provided as described in the specifications.

During the summer of 1887 George W. Freeman did two surveys, one for a wagon road and the other a detailed description of Cape Meares. The U.S. Coast and Geodetic Survey had another survey of both Capes done by Cleveland Rockwell. These reports follow:

LH. 63

Report on a Location
of
Wagon Road
from Tillamook Bay
to Cape Meares Light House Reserv.
by
Geo. W. Freeman
August 1887.

Fort Stevens, Oregon
August 31, 1887
Captain Charles F. Powell
Engineer 13th Light House District
Portland, Oregon

Sir:

In compliance with your verbal instructions, I respectively submit the following report, and estimate of a wagon road from the Sand Spit to the U.S. Lighthouse Reserve at Cape Meares, Oregon. Reference is made to the enclosed sketch.

It is seen by the sketch, that the wagon road would have to start from the extreme northerly point of the Sand Spit and just inside the entrance to Tillamook Bay.

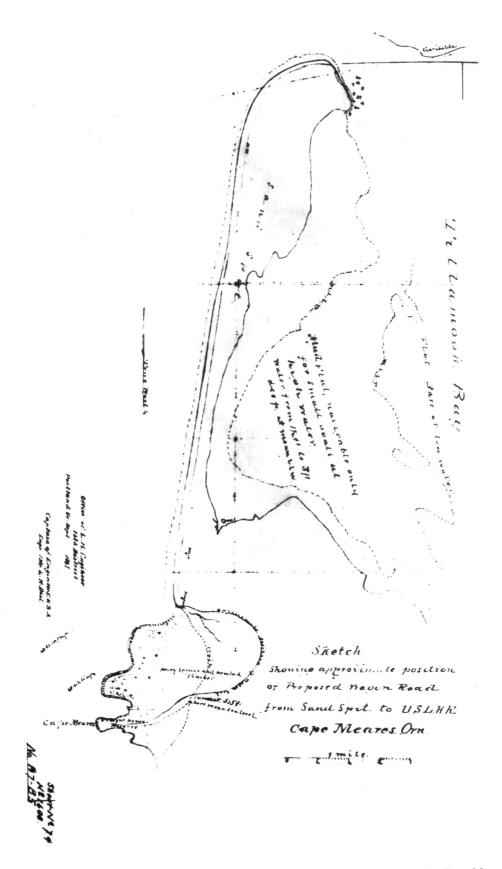

Sketch showing approximate position of Proposed Wagon Road from Sand Spit to U.S.L.H.R., Cape Meares, Orn.

At this point, as is shown on the sketch, the slope of the shore is very steep, and that there is ample water for any steamer or sailing vessel, the size of the *Manzanita* to lay with safety.

From this point the road would have to follow along the beach (the spit, above high water line, being very uneven and covered with loose sand) for a distance of about four miles to a point near the mouth of the small stream, thence following up this stream and along the side hill, to gain distance on account of grade, to the summit, which is 515 feet above main sea level. This distance I have made to be one and one half miles. This gives a grade of 6.5 feet in 100, if this is too steep, possibly a distance of two miles could be made thus reducing the grade to 5 feet in 100 feet.

From the summit to the Light House Reserve a distance of about one half mile the fall is about 10 feet in 100 feet, this however is in the direction of the load and would not therefore be very objectionable.

It would be impossible to land at the head of the little bight, in the inside of Tillamook Bay on account of the vast mud flats which project far into the bay. I think it possible to rig a derrick or tramway on the South side of the Cape, by which the material could be hoisted from a landing stage, constructed below, to the desired point at the top of the Cape. I had no method of reaching the foot of the Cape and could therefore make no examination of the face of the cliff or the depth of water in the immediate vicinity of the Cape, but as far as I could judge from above I think it possible to construct and use some such method.

This landing however could only be used in smooth weather as the Cape faces to the West and therefore is exposed to the direct swell of the ocean.

The region through which the proposed wagon road runs is covered with a heavy growth of spruce and hemlock timber, the earth is a dark loamy soil, mixed with gravel sand and in places clay.

The following estimate explains itself.

Your Obedient Servant,
George W. Freeman
Surveyor U.S.L.E.

Sketch in separate findings.

Estimate of Cost of Proposed Wagon Road from Sand Spit to U.S. Light House Reserve on Cape Meares, Oregon.

Clearing trails, 20 ft. wide, 5 acres @ $5.00 per acre*	$250.00
Removing 8,200 cubic yards of earth @ 20¢ per yard	1,640.00
	$1,890.00
10% for contingencies	189.00
	$2,079.00

George W. Freeman

We believe that the figure should have been $50.00 per acre instead of $5.00

L.H. 64

Report on Survey

of

Cape Meares, Or.

by

Geo. W. Freeman.

August 1887.

Fort Stevens, Oregon
August 24, 1887

Captain Chas. F. Powell
U.S. Lighthouse Engineers
13th District
Portland, Oregon

Sir:

I respectfully submit the following report, together with Field Sheets Nos. 1 & 2 of the survey of Cape Meares, as directed in your letter of July 9th 1887.

Cape Meares is situated about four miles below the entrance to Tillamook Bay, Oregon. A bold rugged headland whose nearly perpendicular sides, vary from two to four hundred feet in height, and whose summit at its highest point is about eight hundred feet above mean sea level.

The Cape taken as a whole is about one mile in width, and projects about one half mile beyond the general coast line.

A very heavy growth of spruce and hemlock timber, with dense salal and salmon berry underbrush covering the main portion of the Cape.

The peninsula that projects nearly due west from the southerly portion of the Cape is covered like the main headland with dense salal and salmon berry underbrush, but the timber is scattering and in small clumps as shown on the Field Sheets.

The peninsula is reached by a trail that branches off to the west near the summit from the main Netarts trail; this latter trail winds up a gulch from the sand spit on the north and crosses the cape at an elevation of 515 feet above mean sea level, thence descends a gulch to short beach, as it is called, on the south.

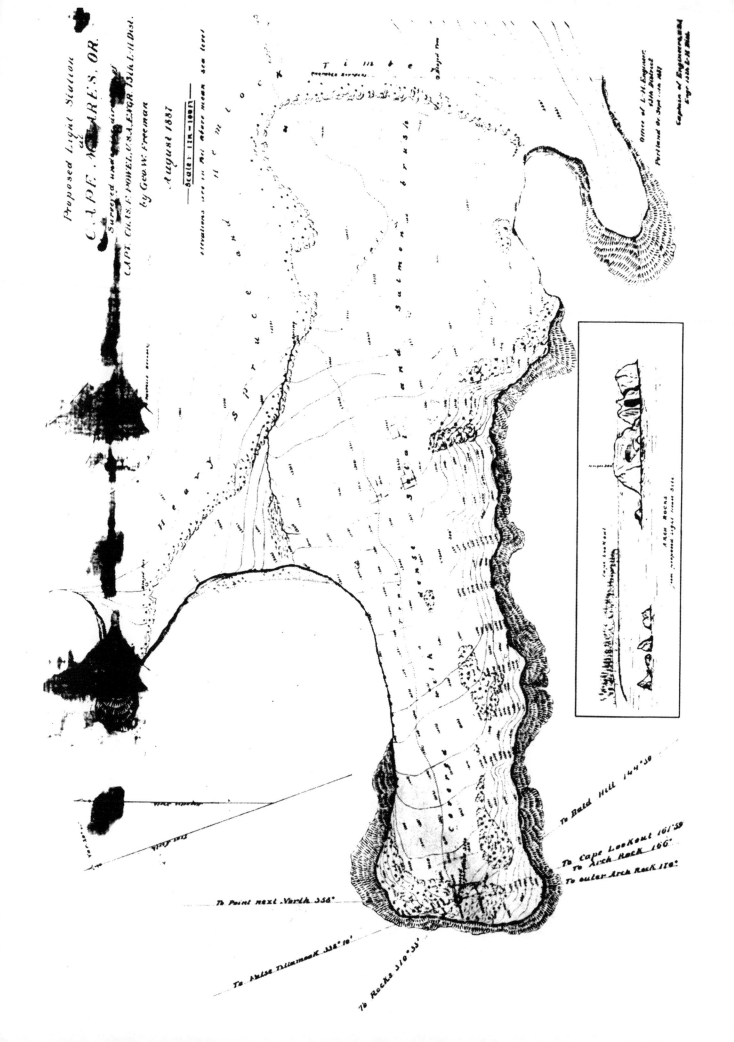

Proposed Light Station at
CAPE MEARES, OR.
Surveyed under direction of
CAPT. CHAS. F. POWEL, U.S.A. ENGR. 13th L.H. Dist.
by Geo. W. Freeman

August 1887

Scale: 1 in = 100 ft

Elevations are in feet above mean sea level

Captain of Engineers and
Engineer 13th L.H. Dist.

Office of L.H. Engineer
13th District
Portland Or. Sept. 15th 1887

To Bald Hill 144° 30'

To Cape Lookout 161° 59'
To Arch Rock 166°
To outer Arch Rock 172°

To Point next North 356°

To False Tillamook 338° 10'

To Rocks 310° 55'

Sheet No. 1 shows the whole tract as surveyed, the boundary lines are located as near as possible to those on the sketch furnished me.

About 350 feet south of where the trail emerges from the timber and about 50 feet east of the line of timber a hemlock 20" in diameter was blazed on four sides, on the west face the letters (E.B./U.S.L.H.R.) were marked in red keel. This marks a point on the east boundary line.

On top of the small knob or projection, about 350 feet north of the swampy ground formed by the outlet to the spring, a hemlock 18" diameter was blazed on four sides, on the south face the letters (N.B./U.S.L.H.R.) were marked in red keel, this marks a point on the north boundary line.

The spring which is marked on Sheet No. 1, is 373 feet above mean sea level, it was extremely difficult to estimate the quantity of flow, as the water stood in pools with no visible connections, in fact from the point where the spring is located to the edge of the bluff (indicated on the sheet by a stream and swamp), no stream was visible. Yet the bed was well marked only a series of pools, there is however a slight seepage over the edge of the bluff. As near as I could estimate by scooping out one of these pools and allowing the water to seep in, the flow is about six gallons per hour, this was in August and of course during the dry season. Probably during the winter the flow is very much more.

The point marked spring on the sheet is the highest point that water was visible, issuing seemingly from the roots of a very large spruce.

The material near the spring is a dark loamy soil to a depth of three or four feet resting upon dark sandstone rock.

The peninsula proper as shown by Sheet No. 2 is about 900 feet long by 250 feet wide on top. At the extreme point it is seen that the slope is to the north, west and south, and at an angle of 25 for a distance of 100.50 to 200 feet then perpendicular to the waters edge.

This point is covered with spruce and hemlock trees from one half to one and a half feet in diameter.

All along the north side, the face of the cliff is nearly perpendicular.

The south side slopes from the even slope of the top at an angle of 25° to 30° for a distance of about 100 feet then perpendicular or nearly so to the waters edge.

The point marked on the sheets as "Proposed light house site" is as far west as is safe in my judgement to go.

This point as is shown on the sheets is 216 feet above mean sea level.

An upper surface of dark loamy soil to the depth of from one half to one and a half feet, then dark sandstone, a sample of which I send you.

No accurate estimate of the annual wear at this point could be made, as the edge could not be reached and examined in safety. As near as I could judge however the wear is very little.

Established near the proposed light-house site on a large hemlock. Elevation 219.92 "

⊙ B.m. 219.19

8'

90°

17'

N 7°32'E

Proposed light house site

US
B.M.
219.92

B.M.

Sketch of Bench Mark

The following sketch show the general outline and relative position of the arch Rock

At the time I made the survey from August 5th to August 11 inclusive with the exception of one day August 11, the cape was enveloped in a dense fog. There was however considerable fog at sea level, it being the foggy season of the year.

The height of the largest was kindly given me by Mr Cleveland Rockwell U.S.C & G. Survey. who was taking coast line in that vicinity and who had more and better facilities than myself for finding the height. The following is a sketch showing the shape etc. of the rocks to the north and west of the proposed light house site. The view was taken at a point about 400 feet west of the proposed light house site

It was impossible to get at the foot of the Cape as the bluff was perpendicular and the peninsula being surrounded by very deep water. The general outline of the bottom was taken as near as possible from various points.

A bench mark was established near the proposed light house site on a large hemlock. Elevation 219.92.

The following sketch show general outline and relative position of the Arch Rock.

The height of the largest was kindly given me by Mr. Cleveland Rockwell, U.S.C. & G. Survey, who was taking coast line in that vicinity and who had more and better facilities than myself for finding the height.

The following is a sketch showing the shape etc. of the rocks to the north and west of the proposed light house site. The view was taken at a point about 400 feet east of the proposed light house site.

Azimuths to these rocks and various points are noted on the sheets. Hoping that the sheets and this report cover all the information asked for.

> I am Yours Respectfully
> Your Obedient Servant
> George W. Freeman
> Surveyor U.S.L.H.E.

Portland, Oregon
U.S. Coast and Geodetic Survey
Portland, Oregon
Sunday August 21, 1887

SPECIAL REPORT

Dr. F. M. Thorn,
Superintendent
Coast and Geodetic Survey
Washington, D.C.

Sir:

I have been informed by Prof. George Davidson, Assistant, that it would be proper for me to make a special report to you upon the adaptability of Cape Lookout and Cape Meares for a Light House site, based upon such information as I could acquire while prosecuting the reconnaissance of the coast in that region. I have the honor therefore to submit the following report with annexed sketches and views:

Cape Lookout is regarded as a more desirable point for a first order Coast light than Cape Meares for the reason that it is more centrally located with respect to the first order Coast lights north and south of it. I would state that if it is desired by the Light House Board to establish a light house at Cape Lookout, there is in my judgement no very formidable reason why they should not do so, and several reasons why it would be a more desirable and useful point than Cape Meares. We will first consider the relative distances between the several points named—Yaquina Point, Cape Lookout, Cape Meares, and Tillamook Rock. The distance from Tillamook Rock and Yaquina Point light house, as taken from the reconnaissance Map No. 603 is 84 miles. The measured distance of Yaquina Point light-house to Cape Lookout from my sheets is 46 miles, thus leaving the distance of Lookout from Tillamook Rock 38 miles; or in other words Cape Lookout is 8 miles nearer Tillamook Rock than it is Yaquina Point.

The distance, Yaquina Point light house to Cape Meares light house site, as measured by me as 56¼ miles, giving us 27¾ miles from Tillamook Rock to Cape Meares and making Cape Meares 28½ miles nearer Tillamook Rock than Yaquina Point. It will thus be seen that a light house at Cape Meares would be one third of the distance from Tillamook to Yaquina Point, a fact worthy of consideration. 2nd. Arcs of Visibility: I regret that at this moment, I have not the time available from field work to construct a map or sketch from my field sheets and other C. and G. Survey data, such as would show clearly the arcs of Visibility of a light placed on either Cape Lookout or Cape Meares, but I am able to make some statement that will show the great disadvantage of Cape Meares in that respect. The southern arc of visibility from Cape Meares in that respect. The southern arc of visibility from Cape Lookout will pass by Cape Foulweather and but 600 metres to the west of the light of Yaquina Point with a clear horizon around the west, passing Cape Meares and commanding the whole Coast line above the mouth of Tillamook Bay to Tillamook Rock. The arc of visibility from Cape Meares would be intercepted by Lookout 10¼ miles distant, and would pass 2½ miles west of the extreme end of Cascade Head, 19 miles south of Lookout. (The distances given in the report are in statute miles). For lack of time as stated above, I cannot now give the distance west of Foulweather this arc would pass. Cape Meares as well as Lookout, commands an unobstructed range of visibility to the northward. In addition to the southern arc of visibility being obstructed by Lookout, the three arch rocks lying off Cape Meares in a direction nearly south, (Compass) distant, one and a half miles or more, would perhaps, considering their height and distance, intercept somewhat the visible arc for, say 7 or 8 degrees, in a direction passing just west of Cape Lookout. There is no arch rock or any other rock around the extremity of Lookout, and I may remark that the arch rock, which is shown and lettered on C. and G.S. Chart No. 603 does not exist and should at once be erased from the plate as liable to mislead. The height of these rocks as determined by me by careful barometer elevations on the shore opposite them and by the hand level and sea horizon is as follows—the inner or north east rock 304 feet—the middle or high arch rock 253 feet and the outer or south west rock 276 feet. The inner rock presents a broad ridge like a house to the end of Meares, the middle rock is rather conical with two apices and the outer rock shows a dome like top.

Difficulties of Construction and Supply

In order to properly examine Cape Lookout (as well as for the purpose of my reconnaissance) I camped on the summit of the Cape on July 19-20 & 21st and on all these days (and many following) though the work could have progressed on the beach, under the fog, nothing could be done on top. The camp was 86* feet above the sea and one and a half miles from the west end, and at this elevation the fog condensed, on everything it touched, dripping from the spruce and hemlock trees like a heavy shower of rain and collecting in streams and pools underneath. The temperature was warm with a light southerly air, the canvas of the tents turned black, pink, yellow and green with the mildew, and stationery, after taking it out of a box would soon fall together like a damp towel. I would remark that the same conditions prevail at all such elevations along the coast. On the 20th July, I made an examination of the end of the Cape. There were no trails except those made by the bear, and the exertion of reaching the end of the Cape and returning is most exhausting, the way being up and down the ravines through dense wet brush through which it is almost impossible to force the way, while tangled windfalls of prostrate large trees could not be penetrated at all without cutting the way with the axe. Bears having steadier heads in steep places than I had would go around these windfalls on the very edge of the precipices. Cape Lookout may be generally described as a bold narrow but high basaltic dyke, projecting into the ocean nearly two miles on a course nearly N.E. and southwest (Magnetic). The width between ends of beaches is but little over one mile and the width at the point is about 400 metres. The south face is very nearly a straight line:—a perpendicular wall of rock from 400 to 800 feet high. The southern edge of this precipice is the highest part of the Cape, the land sloping off to the north. The height across the base is about a thousand feet. The end of the promontory and for one and a half miles back is densely timbered and also covered with the stiffest of salal brush, through which it is scarcely possible to force the way. The extreme south west pinnacle, where I observed the barometer height is 435 feet high; and this is considered too high for a light house. There is however, a projecting base on the south west corner and on the N.W. corner. I consider the southwest corner the proper site for a light house. I did not go down to the waters edge, and indeed I do not think it possible to do so from the top without the aid of ropes, so steep is the slope. I judge the height of the base above the water to be from 100 to 130 feet. The width or space available could not be determined from the summit. I observed the horizontal distance, however, between the cliff

---

* The campsite had to be at least 486 feet high or higher.

at the summit and the base, as seen from Cascade Head, 19 miles distant, to be 170 feet. The site should be examined from a vessel by landing on or near the point. If I could have had a boat or skiff at the end of the rocky beach on the south side, no difficulty would have been found in launching it into the ocean.

There is an excellent anchorage under the south face during the most violent north west winds and the small steamers running to Nestucca Bay often making use of it. The water near the end of the Cape has the appearance from the summit of being very deep, and a vessel properly moored, would have no difficulty in lying close under the rocky walls. I observed that, owing to the depth of water, there would be no ground swell to surge a vessel back and forth, the water appearing to rise and fall gently against the face of the rocks. I think that by commencing on top of the rocky base, a sufficient space could be obtained by blasting away from the slope of the S.W. corner to afford ample room for the lighthouse. From this base the tower would rise to any desired height say 230 feet.

A tramway, the bed of which should be cut out of the sloping beach, could be laid for two or three hundred feet around the south face to a large derrick, or other hoisting apparatus which would lift the material directly from the vessels deck. Previously to commencing operations below, a party should be sent by land to the top of the Cape and shoot off the dangerous rocks at the very summit and all overhanging trees liable to fall and injure property and life. After the light-house was established, the perpetual means of supply would be the same as when constructing. As a matter of course, the construction or the future supplying, could not be done during the prevalence of southerly weather when the sea would render the anchorage untenable. In that respect however, I consider it much easier of construction and maintenance than Tillamook Rock.

A spring of good water, of sufficient supply for domestic use, is found near the end of the Cape not far below the summit and could be brought to the locality in iron pipes.

Cape Meares is a ragged, irregular mass of basaltic rock, projecting half a mile into the ocean with a width between beaches of three fourths of a mile. A short rocky beach separates it from another point of rocks a little over a mile south of the Cape, called (without any sense) Bald mountain,* off which point lie the three arch rocks and many other rocks and ledges, the home of vast numbers of sea lions. The south west point of the Cape is the only available site for a light house and at this place is about 230 feet high.

The ground at the end of this narrow peninsula is well suited for a light house site, being destitute of timber, nearly level on top and covered with a rich soil and a luxuriant and impenetrable growth of salal and salmon berry vines. A good spring of water is found above the proposed site, about 200 meters distant. There is apparently no anchorage under the south side of this point the water appearing to

---

* Now known as Maxwell Mountain and/or Maxwell Point.

be moderately shallow and much swell running in. The difficulties of getting material on the ground would be considerable. A wharf would have to be constructed on Tillamook Bay and a wagon road leading from the wharf to the proposed site, — a distance by the nearest way of about a mile and a quarter. This road would have to be considerably longer in order to make the grade to the lowest pass over the Cape, an elevation of 515 feet. Materials would have to be brought to this wharf on light draft scows, towed in at high water as the upper part of the Bay is a great mud and sand flat. The construction of this wharf and road would be the only difficulty found in constructing and maintaining a light-house at Cape Meares; the site itself being very eligible and pleasant for construction or residence

I append such sketches and views as I feel I have present time to make.

I have the honor to be very respectfully yours

Cleveland Rockwell,
Assistant

Date: 9/14/1887

To: Washington, D.C.

From: Coast and Geodetic Survey

Subject: Cape Meares and Cape Lookout, Oregon. Lighthouse site relative merits report of Asst. Rockwell transmitted.

Apparently the decision to use the Cape Meares site had been made before January 1887 using the information supplied by the Polhemus report of June 1886. It is not known why the U.S. Coast and Geodetic Survey wanted another survey conducted.

Contrary to the legends that abound about the misplaced lighthouse, it is obvious from the above reports that they knew exactly where and why the lighthouse was going to be built. Even though Rockwell's report favored Cape Lookout as a better location as far as visibility and position was concerned, there was no question that Cape Meares was a more practical choice. Transporting materials for

building and later for maintaining the station were far easier and much less costly at the chosen site.

Through some misunderstanding, the Coast Survey adopted the name Cape Lookout for the long narrow headland that juts two and one-half miles out into the sea ten miles south of its northern neighbor also known as Cape Lookout. It appeared as such on the charts of 1850 and 1853. In 1857 George Davidson of the U.S. Coast and Geodetic Survey renamed the northern most headland Cape Meares in honor of its early discoverer. This was done because serious navigational errors were occurring and there was concern that during poor visibility a vessel could mistake the shallow bar of Netarts Bay with the deeper, safer entrance at Tillamook Bay which was just 7.8 miles north of Cape Meares

Confusion over which Cape was which lasted for years when mariners continued using outdated charts. The mix-up has lasted into the 20th century.

The legend that the Cape Meares Lighthouse was built on the wrong cape can still be heard today.

Date: 12/28/1887

To: 13th District

From: Engineer Powell

Subject: Cape Meares, Oregon. Tracings of proposed location of tower. Preparations of plans and specifications by Board asked.

Date: 12/29/1887

To: 13th District

From: Engineer Powell

Subject: Cape Meares, Oregon. Characteristics of Light. Recommendations.

Date: 1/31/1888

To: Lighthouse Board

From: Engineering Committee

Subject: Cape Meares, Oregon. Plans approved and recommended.

Two local loggers were subcontracted to do the hauling from the bay up to the lighthouse site. A lighthouse tender brought the materials and supplies into Tillamook Bay where they were off-loaded onto a scow. The scow delivered its load to the south end of the Tillamook Bay spit near the old Hauxhurst place. Myron Perkins and Bill Johnson brought their teams of horses and four or five yoke of oxen from their logging operations across the bay to the landing site. They did all the hauling of building materials to the station until the connecting link to Hodgdon Road was finished in 1893.

A log is hooked up to six yoke of oxen working along Tillamook Bay, circa 1885.

Date: 7/20/1888
To: 12th District
From: Engineer Handberg
Subject: Cape Meares, Oregon. Construction advertising proposals
   fixed, date for completion of contracts reported.

Date: 9/7/1888
To: 13th District
From: Engineer Handberg
Subject: Cape Meares, Oregon. Metal work, etc. contract
   award to lowest Bidder Recommended.

Building the Tower

The sheet iron work for the tower was done by the Willamet (Willamette) Iron Works of Portland, Oregon and transported to Tillamook by ship. It was hauled up the wagon road and delivered to the site on March 1, 1889 at a cost of $7,800. Charles B. Duhrkoop of Portland was in charge of the tower erection.

Plans required that the iron tower be lined with brick. Mr. Duhrkoop found that the difficulty and expense of transporting brick to the site was prohibitive, so a search of the Cape was made to locate a suitable source of clay. When clay was found near the station site, he built a kiln. Local Indians were hired to dig the clay and cut the timber needed to fire the kiln. Enough brick was made at the Cape to supply the construction needs of all the buildings erected at the station. On completion of the tower job on September 24, 1889, he was paid $2,900.

Charles B. Duhrkoop was born in Hamburg, Germany, November 13, 1830. He died in Portland, Oregon on January 9, 1893 of pneumonia and is buried in the Riverview Cemetery in Portland.

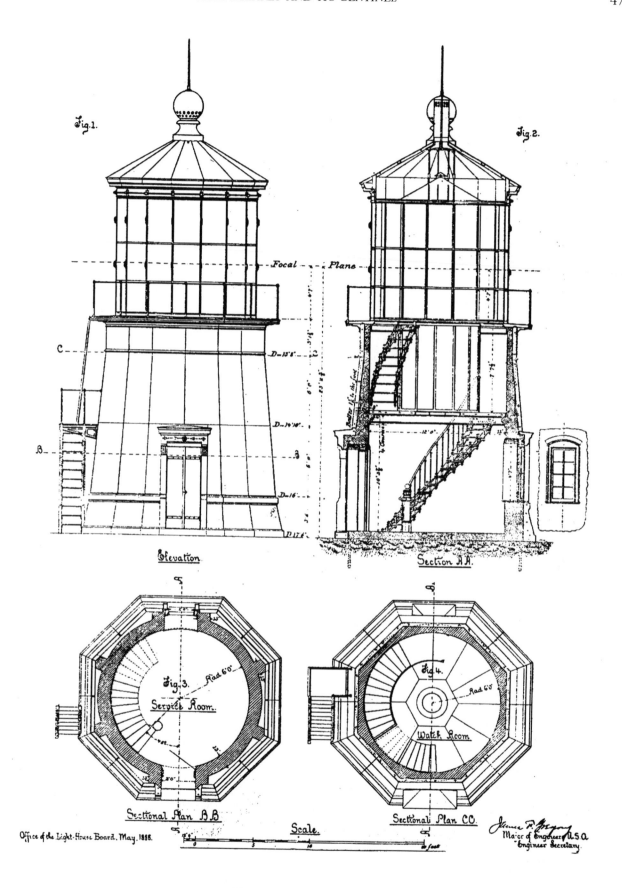

Plans for the tower, May 1888.

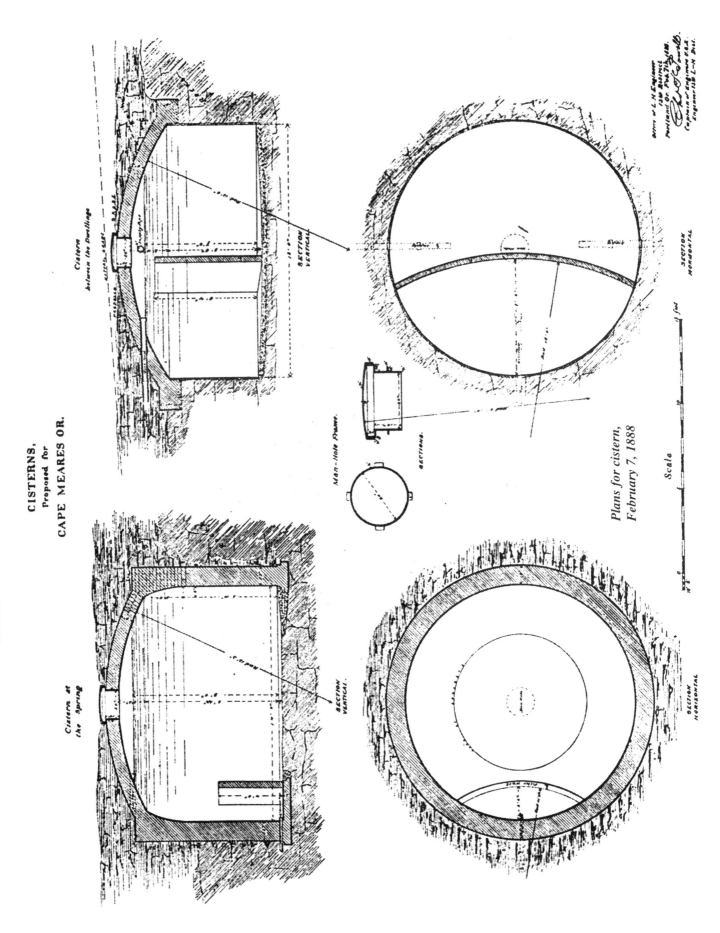

CAPE MEARES LIGHT-STATION, OR.

CISTERNS,
Proposed for
CAPE MEARES OR.

*Plans for cistern,
February 7, 1888*

Date: 10/16/1888
To: Treasury Department
From: Secretary of Treasury
Subject: Cape Meares, Oregon. Construction of buildings, cistern,
        draining and grading grounds. Contract authorized.

Date: 11/13/1888
To: Treasury Department
From: Secretary of Treasury
Subject: Cape Meares, Oregon. Obtaining land for Lighthouse.
        Tracings of official survey forwarded

Date: 5/9/1889
To: Lighthouse Board
From: Committee on location
Subject: Additional land reservation for Lighthouse purposes
recommended.

Date: 6/23/1889
To: 3rd District
From: Engineer Heap
Subject: Cape Meares, Oregon. Illuminating apparatus 1st Order
        shipment reported.

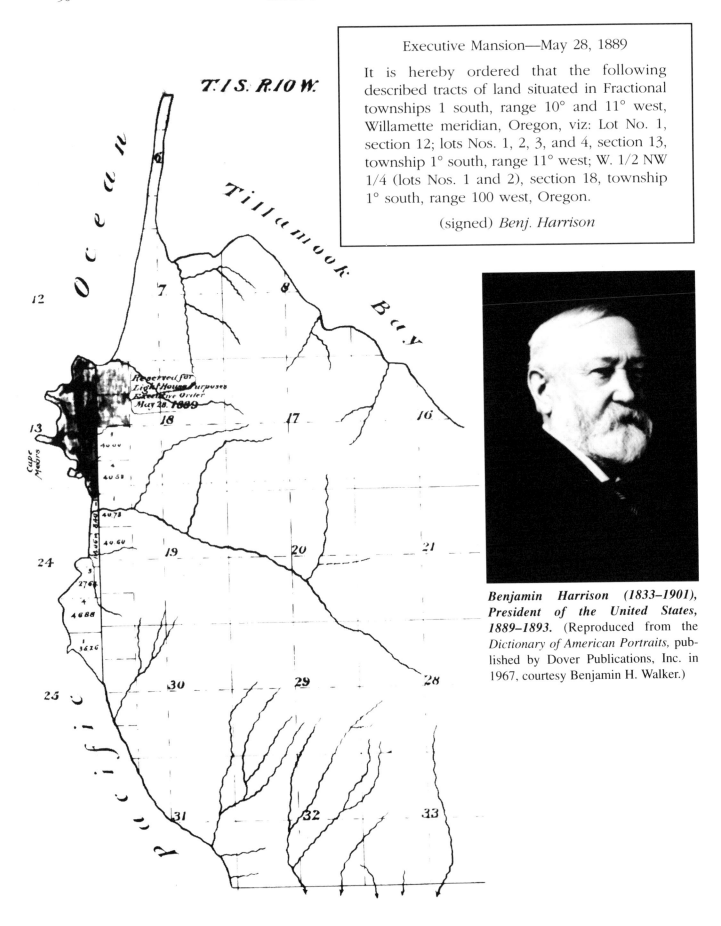

T. 1 S. R. 10 W.

Executive Mansion—May 28, 1889

It is hereby ordered that the following described tracts of land situated in Fractional townships 1 south, range 10° and 11° west, Willamette meridian, Oregon, viz: Lot No. 1, section 12; lots Nos. 1, 2, 3, and 4, section 13, township 1° south, range 11° west; W. 1/2 NW 1/4 (lots Nos. 1 and 2), section 18, township 1° south, range 100 west, Oregon.

(signed) *Benj. Harrison*

Benjamin Harrison (1833–1901), President of the United States, 1889–1893. (Reproduced from the *Dictionary of American Portraits*, published by Dover Publications, Inc. in 1967, courtesy Benjamin H. Walker.)

The Light
What Lighthouses are all About

French physicist Augustin Fresnel (fra-nell) perfected the design of the lens that bears his name in 1822. The giant beehive structure revolutionized the lighting of lighthouses and is used worldwide. Henry LePaute of Paris, France, hand ground the glass and constructed the lens for Cape Meares in 1887.

The outer surface of the eight-sided lens is made of curved prisms that refract or bend the light so that it comes from the center of the apparatus in a narrow sheet. Four powerful magnifying glasses (bull's-eyes) placed at the center of the lens intensifies the light resulting in a bright horizontal beam of concentrated light. The bull's-eye panels alternate with the plain panels.

The original illumination came from a kerosene burning Funck float lamp that had five tubular wicks, fitting but not touching, inside each other. The outside wick was four and 5/16 inches in diameter. The lamp was attached to a stationary post mounted in the center of the huge lens. The light of the lamp was aligned with the center of the bull's-eyes. The station kept one spare lamp and three spare burners for emergencies. The lantern was so large that the keepers could walk around on metal grating on the inside as well as the outside of the lens when doing their daily cleaning. The entire apparatus was enclosed by 48 protective glass panels.

Close-up of Cape Meares light with canvas curtains to protect prisms from the intense sunlight.

The name plate that Henry LePaute attached to the lantern post in 1887 was stolen sometime after 1964. This photo was taken in 1950. No questions would be asked if it were returned to the Tillamook County Pioneer Museum.

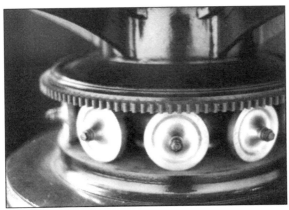

Wheels of the chariot (rotating clockwork mechanism) as they look today.

Lantern post as it appeared in 1989.

Close-up of brass mountings that hold prisms.

This enormous device is twelve feet tall and six feet wide and weighs over 2,000 pounds. When it was operational, it completed one revolution every four minutes. As it turned, the fixed white light of the lamp shone through the clear panels of the lantern and developed 18,000 candlepower

of light. Four (hinged for cleaning) ruby-red panels of glass were fastened to the outside frame of the lantern in front of the bull's-eyes, and to equalize visibility, produced 160,000 candlepower of red light. The intervals between red flashes were one minute with a duration of about five seconds

The clockwork mechanism housed in the base of the pedestal was a chariot with ten brass wheels, five inches in diameter and 7/8 inch thick, traveling in a 22-inch diameter circle. There were two rows of guide wheels revolving horizontally around the center column. The cord led from the drum in the pedestal over the traveling sheave (grooved wheel) and through the pulley on the weight back to the pedestal where the end was secured. The weight was suspended vertically below the pedestal. The length of the drop was 10 ft. 1 in. through the tube into the workroom

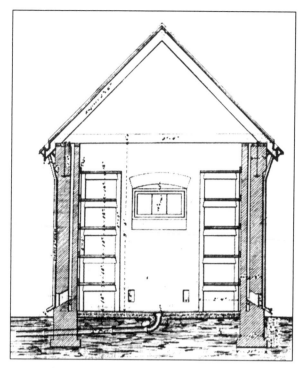

Store house for mineral oil—December 28, 1887.

the point where it had to be reset, the piece of wood would gently touch them, wakening them in time to rewind the mechanism before the lens stopped turning.

The huge Fresnel lens was shipped from Paris, sailed the Atlantic, through the Straits of Magellan at the tip of South America then north along the Pacific coast to Tillamook. On the southwest tip of the Cape, a large hand-operated derrick with a long boom was constructed of Sitka spruce timber cut on the site. After the ship arrived and the weather cooperated enough for it to maneuver close to the Cape, the lens was hoisted from the deck up the face of the cliff, over 200 feet, into the waiting tower.

The tower at Cape Meares is 36 feet high, focal plane elevation 223 feet, visibility 21 miles.

Preparation of building plans began in the summer of 1887. Specifications were recommended. Approvals were authorized. Contracts were advertised then awarded. Work was begun and completed. Inspections were made. Recommendations for payments were requested. Penalties were imposed if deliveries were late and/or contracts ran overtime. Payments were made.

below. The machinery would run 2 hours and 30 minutes on one winding.

Even though strictly forbidden, keepers were known to catnap during quiet nights by fastening a small piece of wood horizontally to the bottom of the weight and positioning themselves directly below it. When the weight gradually dropped to

The following information deals with the major contractors:

File No.:	1862	1863	1864
Date of Contract:	27 September, 1888	24 September, 1888	2 October, 1888
Contracting Parties:	Willamet Iron Works Portland, Oregon	Chas. B. Duhrkoop Portland, Oregon	Richard Seaman Portland, Oregon
Subject of Contract:	Cape Meares, OR Metal Work for Tower	Cape Meares, OR Erection of Tower	Cape Meares, OR Buildings, Gradings, etc.
When to be Delivered:	1 March, 1889	26 June, 1889	31 March, 1889 15 August, 1889
Where:	Cape Meares, OR	Cape Meares, OR	Cape Meares, OR
Period:	1889	1889	1889
Price:	$7,800.00	$2,900.00	$33,829.00
When to be Paid:	In three installments	Upon Completion	In 3 installments (see instructions to bidders)

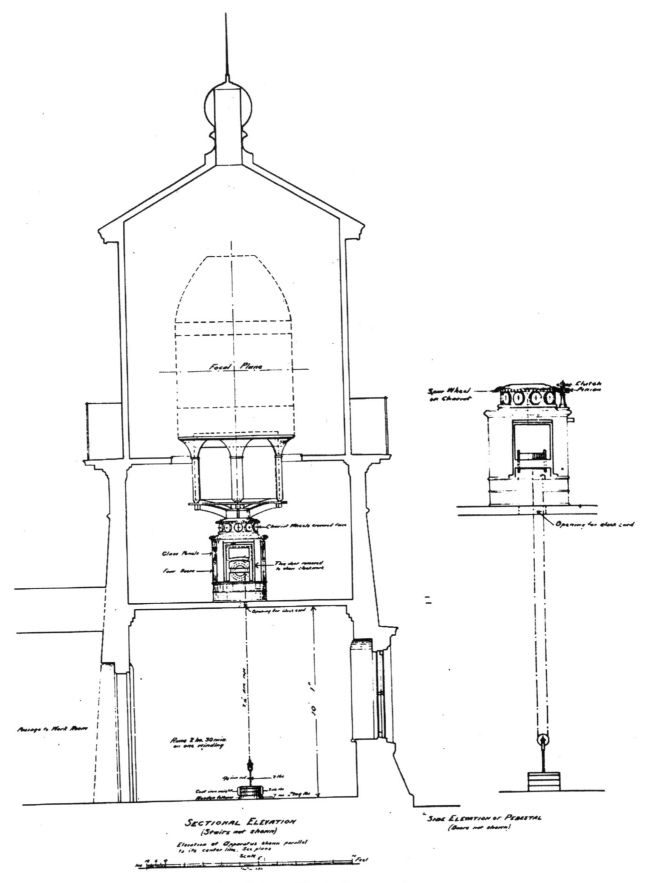

Installation of illuminating apparatus

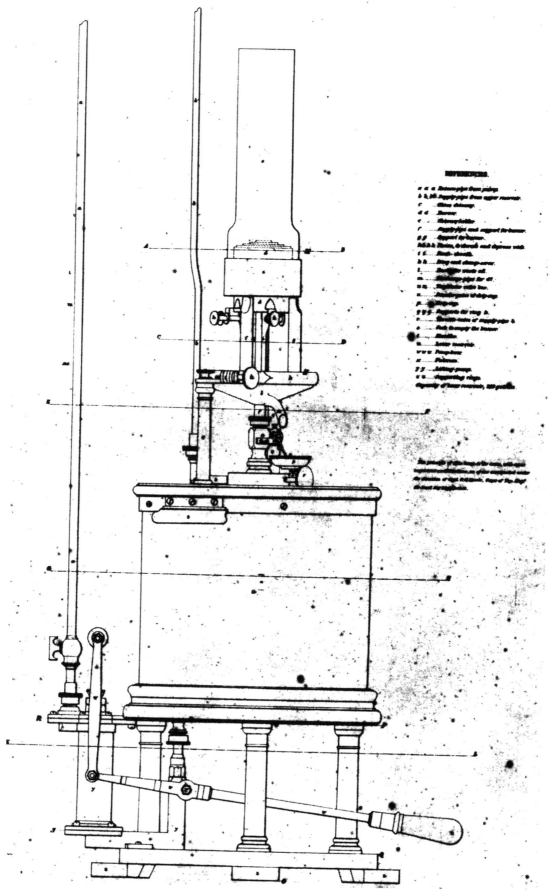

First Order Hydraulic Lamp. Plate 14-1, Volume 15

First Order Catadioptric Lens Apparatus

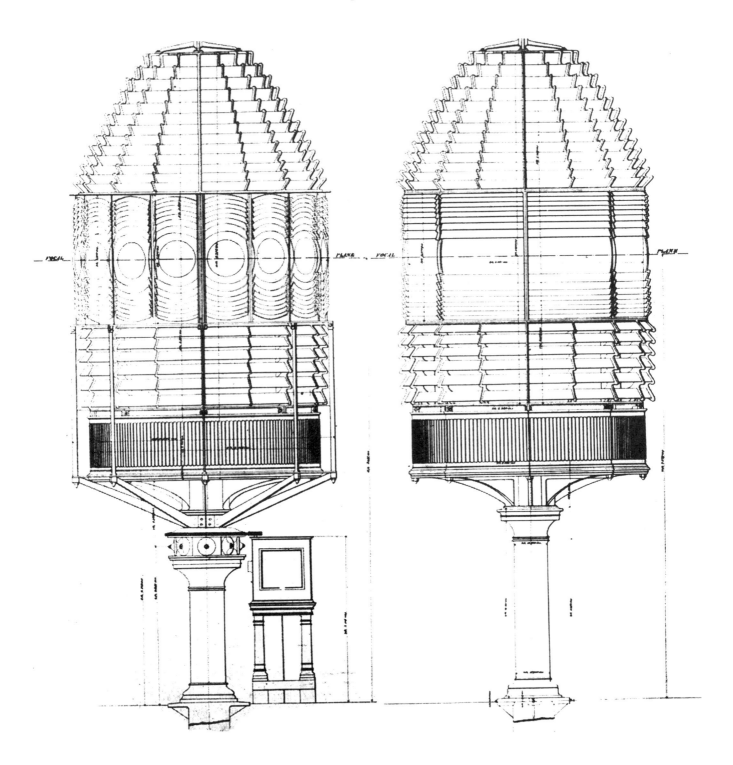

Flashes every thirty seconds.   **Fixed Light**

Date: 10/2/1889
To: 13th District
From: Engineer Handberg
Subject: Cape Meares, Oregon. Lighthouse work near completion —
appointment of Keeper suggested.

Date: 11/18/1889
To: 13th District
From: Engineer Handberg
Subject: Cape Meares, Oregon. Light data for "Notice to Marines":
suggestions as to illuminating apparatus.

Date: 12/2/1889
To: 13th District
From: Engineer Handberg
Subject: Cape Meares, Oregon. Funds on hand to pay all expenses
— including transportation & supplies.

Date: 12/28/1889
To: 13th District
From: Engineer Handberg
Subject: Cape Meares, Oregon. Completion date of lighthouse
reported.

NOTICE TO MARINERS.

(No. 71, of 1889.)

UNITED STATES OF AMERICA—OREGON.

Light at Cape Meares.

Notice is hereby given that, on or about January 1, 1890, a fixed white light of the first order, varied by a red flash every minute, will be shown from the structure recently erected on the extreme westerly end of Cape Meares, Oregon.

The light will illuminate the entire horizon.

The focal plane is 223 feet above mean sea-level, and the light may be seen, in clear weather, from the deck of a vessel 15 feet above the sea, 21¼ nautical miles.

The light is shown from a black lantern surmounting a low white tower in form of a frustum of an octagonal pyramid.

Two brown oil-houses (distant 65 feet) and a keeper's dwelling, painted white with lead-colored trimmings and brown roofs (distant 1,000 feet), stand to the eastward of the tower.

The approximate geographical position of the light-house, as taken from the charts of the U. S. Coast and Geodetic Survey, is as follows:

Latitude,   45° 28′ (52″) North.
Longitude, 123° 58′ (30″) West.

Magnetic bearings and distances of prominent objects are approximately as follows:

Tillamook Rock Light-House, N. N. W. ¼ W., 27¼ nautical miles.
Cape Lookout, S. by E., 9 nautical miles.

Cape Foulweather Light is the next light to the southward, distant 49 miles.

BY ORDER OF THE LIGHT-HOUSE BOARD:

DAVID B. HARMONY,
Rear-Admiral U. S. Navy,
Chairman.

OFFICE OF THE LIGHT-HOUSE BOARD,
Washington, D. C., December 2, 1889.

...edication ceremonies on January 1, 1890 were attended by uniformed members of the U.S. Army Corp of Engineers. This is the oldest ...own photo of the Lighthouse and is printed from an 8x10 glass plate negative in the Tillamook County Pioneer Museum's photo collec-...n. Photographer unknown.

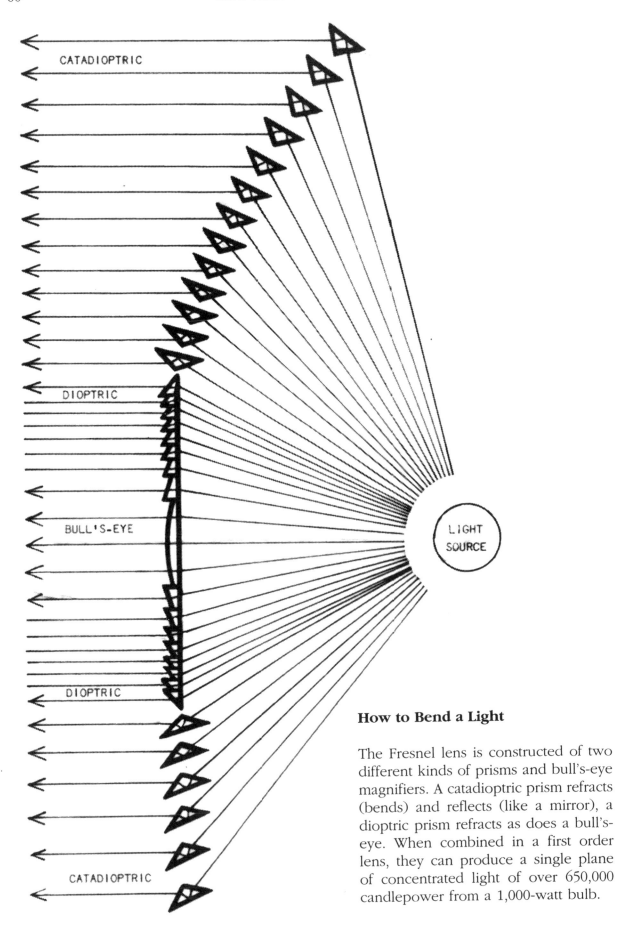

CATADIOPTRIC

DIOPTRIC

BULL'S-EYE

DIOPTRIC

CATADIOPTRIC

LIGHT SOURCE

How to Bend a Light

The Fresnel lens is constructed of two different kinds of prisms and bull's-eye magnifiers. A catadioptric prism refracts (bends) and reflects (like a mirror), a dioptric prism refracts as does a bull's-eye. When combined in a first order lens, they can produce a single plane of concentrated light of over 650,000 candlepower from a 1,000-watt bulb.

The Keepers

The main tasks of the Keeper and his assistants were to operate the light from sunset to sunrise and to keep the lighting equipment in good condition. These tasks were spelled out in precise detail by the Lighthouse Board. Keepers had to know how to read the "Instructions and Directions" manuals that covered every phase of lighthouse keeping—daily and periodic as:

Have the lantern and lens in order by ten o'clock in the morning for lighting in the evening. When more than one keeper was at a station, duties were divided. On a normal day the keeper performing "first department" work would clean and polish the lens, clean and fill the lamp, dust the framework of the apparatus, carefully trim the wicks of the lens lamp, and if required, put new ones in, and see that everything connected with the apparatus and lamp in general was perfectly clean and the lamp ready for lighting in the evening.

The keeper assigned to "second department" duties had to clean the copper and brass fixtures of the apparatus as well as the utensils used in the lantern and watch room; clean the walls, floors, and balconies, or galleries of the lantern; sweep and dust the tower stairways, landing, doors, windows, window recesses, and passageways from the lantern to the oil storage area. Linen aprons were to be worn over their clothes to prevent the possibility of their coarse clothing scratching the lens.

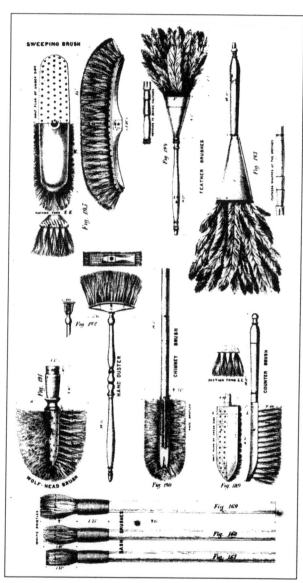

Just a sampling of a Keeper's tools: sweeping brush, feather brushes, hand duster, chimney brush, counter brush, wolf-head brush, and sash brushes.

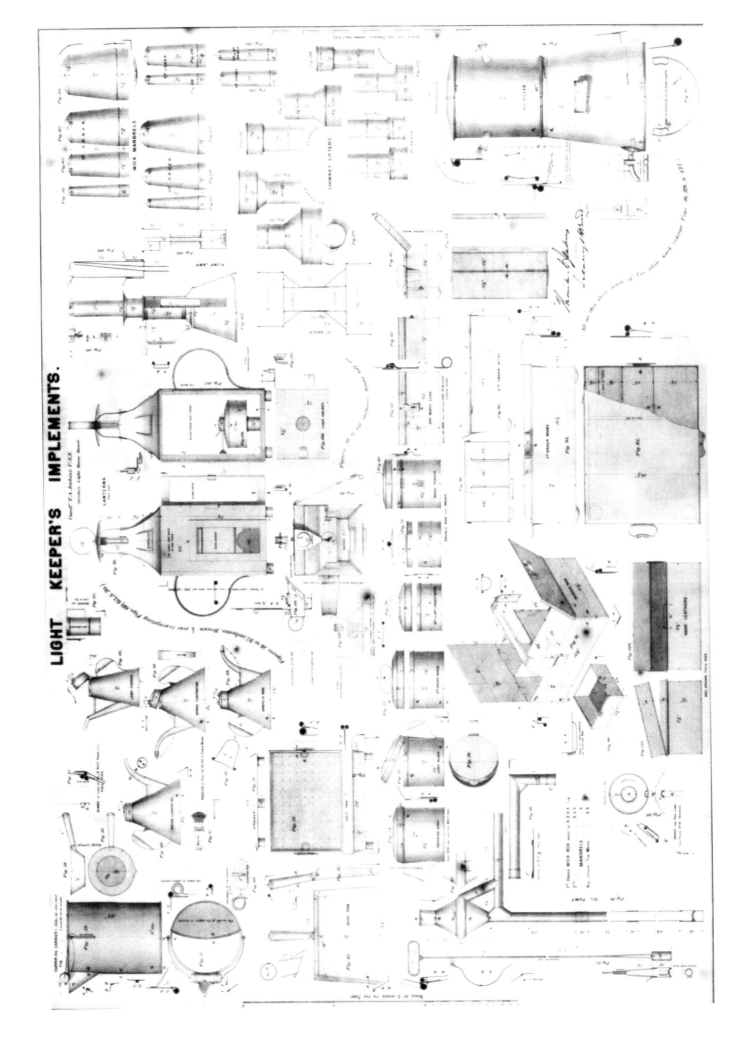

LIGHT KEEPER'S IMPLEMENTS.

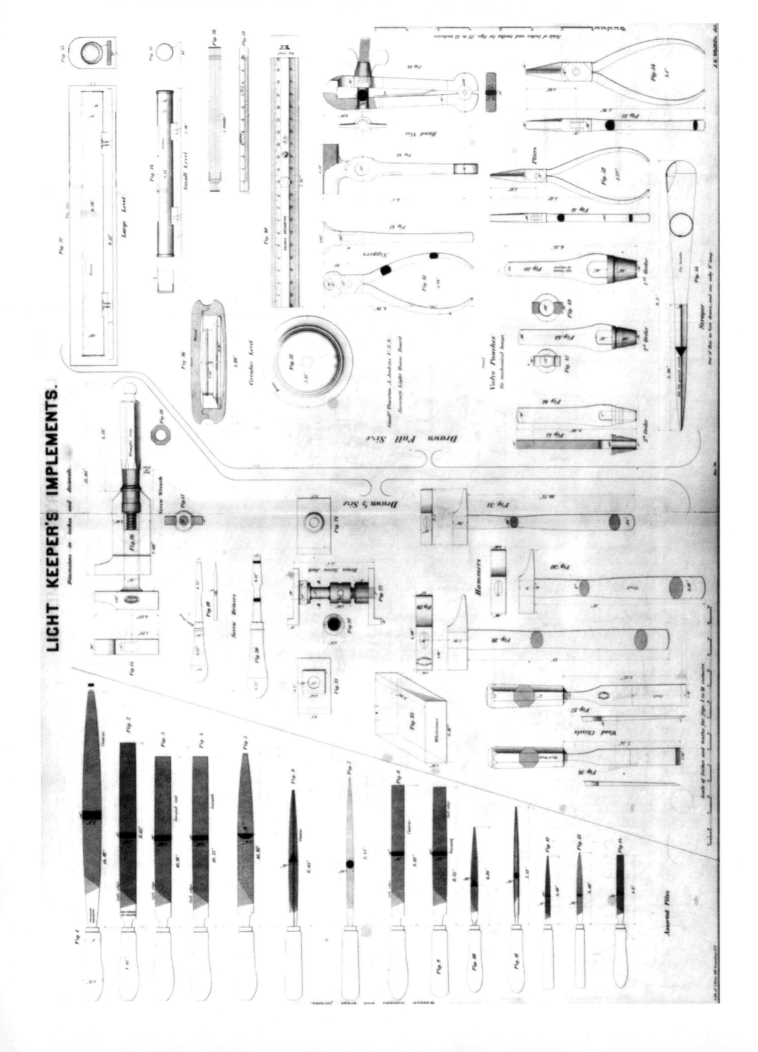

LIGHT KEEPER'S IMPLEMENTS.

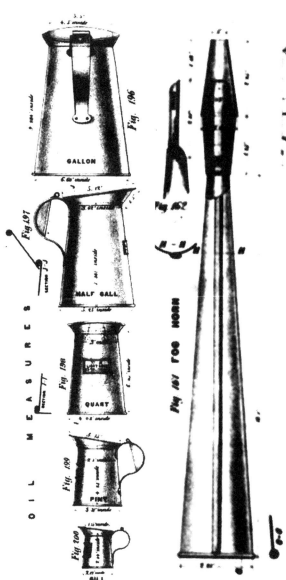

Oil measures: gallon, half gallon, quart, pint, gill; fog horn.

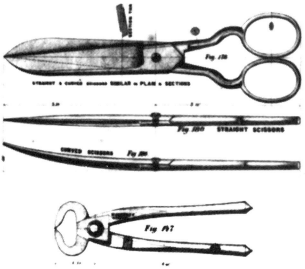

Straight and curved scissors, glaziers pincers.

After the daily routines were finished, there were instructions on how to maintain and make repairs on the equipment and structures at the station. Keeping the tower painted was no small chore. If major trouble developed, arrangements were made with the district engineer for repairs or replacement. Quarterly inspections assured a neat and well-kept station.

When time would allow, many keepers would engage in outside occupations to relieve boredom and supplement their income. Families often participated in these undertakings. Fishing and hunting were ideal activities as they also varied the family diet.

Periodic routines were detailed in other books. These directed them on how to do such things as wash the lens every two months with spirit of wine (alcohol), polish it annually with rouge, and alternate the lamps inside the lens every fifteen days. If oil was dripped on the lens, there were instructions on how to clean it off with spirits of wine. There were books with detailed illustrations on how to trim and adjust a wick and what the flame in the lamp should look like.

EARLY KEEPERS

Anthony W. Miller, Keeper, appointed
    November 26, 1889.
Andrew Hold, First Assistant Keeper,
    appointed November 26, 1889.
Henry York, Second Assistant Keeper,
    appointed November 26, 1889.
Daniel R. Hurlbut, Second Assistant
    Keeper, appointed December 3, 1891.
George Hunt, Keeper, appointed January
    30, 1892.
Daniel R. Hurlbut, First Assistant Keeper,
    appointed March 8, 1894.

Edward A. Brooks, Second Assistant
Keeper, appointed March 8, 1894.
George W. Boyington, Second Assistant
Keeper, appointed February 1, 1898.
Hermann Grossheim, First Assistant
Keeper, appointed February 2, 1900.
George H. Higgins, Second Assistant
Keeper, appointed January 1, 1901.
Andrew Jackson, First Assistant Keeper,
appointed February 26, 1902.
George Higgins, First Assistant Keeper,
appointed May 1, 1903.
Samuel B. Morris, Second Assistant
Keeper, appointed June 12, 1903.
Mrs. Augusta Hunt, Acting Keeper,
appointed July 11, 1903 to August 14,
1903.
Harry D. Mahler, Keeper, appointed
August 3, 1903.
Patrick Murphy, Second Assistant Keeper,
appointed March 5, 1906.

Daniel R. and Catherine Hurlbut taken when he was First Assistant Keeper at Cape Meares, circa 1895.

Jacob Ericksen, Second Assistant Keeper,
appointed October 10, 1906.
George H. Higgins, Keeper, appointed
July 1, 1907.
Gus Jansen, First Assistant Keeper,
appointed August 1, 1907.
Thomas P. Ford, Keeper, appointed
December 1, 1909.
John Matela, Second Assistant Keeper,
appointed September 1, 1910.

Their Families

The Keepers had daily routines and chores to keep them busy. Their families often found the isolation and solitude difficult to live with and loneliness and monotony were the words they most often used to describe their lives.

First Assistant Keeper Andrew Hold served at Cape Meares from November 26, 1889 to March 8, 1894.

George H. Hunt was appointed Keeper at Cape Meares on January 30, 1892.

Cape to the village of Barnegat at the southwest end of Tillamook Bay. The boat, kept in a rough boathouse built by the keepers, would then be taken into town. These trips were carefully timed to sail at half tide or higher, when water covered the mud flats of the bay. Prior to the completion of the road to Netarts and then to Tillamook, packhorses were often used to transport freight when the road to the bay was too muddy.

The Lighthouse Board began distributing small libraries to the more isolated lighthouses in 1876. There were about 40 different books in each cased set. The mixture contained novels, histories, biographies, adventures, religious works and magazines.

At Cape Meares the Keepers and their families maintained a large garden (6/10 of an acre) in the rich loamy soil. It was enclosed in a wire mesh fence to keep the deer out. Altogether, 1-1/3 acres were fenced at the station. Heavy timber rose behind the dwellings to the east. There was one barn, one woodshed, three poultry houses and one privy. Besides the poultry, a cow and several horses were kept at the station. Tending the garden and animals occupied a lot of their time.

The two large dwellings were painted white with gray trimming and brown roofs. They were surrounded by a white picket fence. Plank walks extended around the houses and to the other buildings and down the 10° slope, 1,000 feet west to the tower.

Trips to Tillamook City were rare occasions for the families. They would travel the two miles northeast down the

George H. Higgins, Second Assistant Keeper at Cape Meares, was married to Amelia M. Freeman, daughter of L.G. Freeman, an early Tillamook pioneer, at the Lighthouse Station on December 25, 1901. They had four children, three of whom were born at the Cape.

(Top) George and Augusta Boyington with daughters Alice and Hazel. Lady seated on steps is Mable E. Larr, 1898. (Right) Mrs. Augusta Boyington Hunt (1937). Widowed in 1899, she married Keeper George Hunt in April, 1903 and became Acting Keeper on July 11, 1903 for one month when George died suddenly.

They were exchanged about every six months. These circulating libraries were still in use as late as 1912.

Families often pitched in to help with lighthouse chores. On a number of occasions wives were appointed to the post of Keeper when their husbands became ill or died. At Cape Meares this happened to Mrs. Augusta Hunt on July 11, 1903.

Harry D. Mahler was appointed Keeper on August 3, 1903. There is no better way to get the feel of living at the station for children than by reading of their own experiences. Mahler had three children when he transferred to Cape Meares from Alki Point Lighthouse in Puget

Keeper Harry D. Mahler and his family in the summer of 1906. Louise Mahler, his wife, Frances standing, Margaret and Howard. Taken beside the lighthouse at Cape Meares.

Sound. The children were Howard, Frances and Margaret. This account was written by Frances LePoividen and Margaret White in 1976 and is included with their kind permission.

"In 1903 our father was transferred to Cape Meares. The Cape Meares lighthouse is unique. It is an eight-sided cage of glass, each prismatic glass section was ground in France and transported to Cape Meares. It is also possible to walk around on the inside of the lens as well as on the outside. There are only two lighthouses in the world where it is possible to do this.

"At Cape Meares we went to school for the first time. The first year we had three months of schooling, after that we had four months each year. It was three-quarters of a mile to the school down a very steep hill and then along the beach. We children all piled on one horse for the trip. Sometimes, after a rain, it was very slippery going down the hill. When this happened the wise old horse scrunched down on his haunches and slid. We loved it and would squeal with pleasure and hang on for dear life.

"There were five children in the one room school which was heated by a big stove. The teacher boarded with us when school was in session.

"We always had a huge garden and at Cape Meares we had a cow. Shopping at Cape Meares was complicated. We went to market in Tillamook. Everything was bought in large quantities, mostly staples

(Above) Frances, Howard and Margaret Mahler playing house in 1904. (Right) Howard, Margaret and Frances Mahler in 1906.

The Mahler children, Frances, Howard an dMargaret, had just returned from vacation in Seattle and were playing "news boys" in 1907.

and dried foods, and everything was stored in huge watertight containers.

"We left Cape Meares by boat at high tide and hurried to get back before the tide changed. Sometimes we were too late and the boat had to be pulled over the mud flats on rollers. This was a messy, sticky chore and father was thankful for the assistance of an Indian named Ezra who was always there to help pull.

"Of course there was no radio or TV in those days; we made our own fun using our imagination. Our doll houses were made of logs and our dolls of rags. We used to catch wood toads to eat the insects in the garden. We would crawl to the edge of the promontory to look down at the birds' nests 350 feet below. Our poor mother must have held her breath many times as her fearless children hung over the cliff.

"A near tragedy happened one day when Margaret was standing on a log that was being sawed. She slipped and fell behind her brother just as he brought down his double bitted ax. There was a large gash in her forehead. The only thing Mother had to stop the blood was cotton which was liberally applied to the wound. This was not a very good idea and removing it at the doctor's office was exceedingly painful. Mother and Margaret were taken to Tillamook by buggy. It was a hazardous, excruciating all-night ride. The doctor, after removing the cotton, put a piece of tape on each side of the wound and sewed it together. He did a wonderful job and it healed without a scar.

"There were lots of sea lions at Cape Meares. The sea lion cry is so human-sounding that Mother would get up during the night thinking something was wrong with one of us children.

(Top) All ready for the four months of school in 1906. On the first horse is Miss Endicott, the teacher who roomed and boarded with the Mahler family. Behind her are the daughters of Second Assistant Keeper S.B. Morris. On the second horse are Howard, Margaret and Frances Mahler. It was approximately a mile by the north trail to the school. (Left) Harry D. Mahler (1864–1935), then Keeper at Alki Point Lightstation. He retired at age 66 after 42 years in the Lighthouse Service on November 1, 1930

There were also lots of bears at Cape Meares, but they were afraid of us and would amble away when we came by. Father caught a bear in a trap and his pelt made a nice rug for us children.

(Facing page) Certificate awarded to Keeper Harry D. Mahler for "Valuable Services" at the Lewis and Clark Centennial Exposition 1905 and American Pacific Exposition and Oriental Fair, Portland, Oregon. The original is in the Tillamook County Pioneer Museum's collections.

Lighthouse Visitors

No one was more welcome than the rare visitor to this remote and isolated station. Getting there and back took a full day, whether by boat or wagon and fair weather was a necessity. The following is an account by Carol Phillips Spring:

"In 1900 we used to drive our team of horses and wagon, empty save for our lunch, right up over the unmarked trail over the Mountain from what is now called Oceanside. We just called it Maxwells Point then, all the rest was Netarts.

(Top left) Gust, Mimmi and Albert Jansen, circa 1914. (Top right) Keeper Gust Jansen and guests enjoy a sunny summer day, 1924. (Lower right) Albert Jansen on porch of Keeper's house, circa 1914.

(Top left) Jessie Miller, top, Dora Witt and Ida Buckner were summer visitors, 1915. (Top right) Group of visitors, circa 1900. (Lower right) Charlie Miller kneeling, in front from left Amy Stranahan and daughters Shirley and Marbeth, and Cora Miller, 1926.

"When we had eaten lunch en route and, after a hard climb, had finally reached the houses above the lighthouse, we were warmly welcomed by the lonely, isolated people who lived there. They took us into their parlor and gave us wonderful stereopticon views to look at. These were pioneers in the three dimensional fields, and were charming to us.

"When we reached the lighthouse itself, the affable keeper let us children ride on the revolving platform around the great kerosene lamp. He told us how many times the kerosene was strained for the lamp, the last straining thru fine silk. The trimming of the great tubular wick, was no small chore."

These occasions were delightful events for all, especially for the keepers and their families. As the roads improved, the isolation diminished.

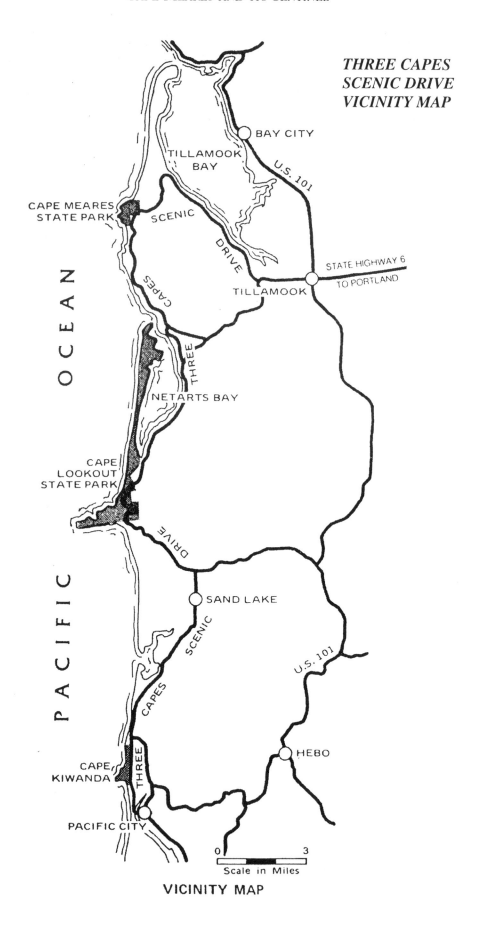

**THREE CAPES
SCENIC DRIVE
VICINITY MAP**

BAY CITY

TILLAMOOK
BAY

U.S. 101

CAPE MEARES
STATE PARK

SCENIC

DRIVE

CAPES

STATE HIGHWAY 6
TO PORTLAND

TILLAMOOK

O C E A N

THREE

NETARTS BAY

CAPE
LOOKOUT
STATE PARK

DRIVE

P A C I F I C

SAND LAKE

SCENIC

U.S. 101

CAPES

HEBO

THREE

CAPE
KIWANDA

PACIFIC CITY

0   3
Scale in Miles

VICINITY MAP

Coast Guardsmen Keepers

Clockwise, top left: Keeper Archie Cameron and his wife, Pricilla, 1948; Keeper William Frazier on a foggy day, 1948; Assistant Keeper William R. Christensen on left, Keeper William Frazier, 1948; Mrs. Vivian Frazier and daughter Willow, 1948. Here they're pictured beside the storage-power building which held one 3 KVA generator and two 5 KVA generators.

Jerry Cook, Assistant Keeper Mel Cook, Keeper Archie Cameron with Barbara Ann Cook in front and Colleen Cameron, 1949.

Keepers and visitors inside the tower, 1948.

Keeper Bill Covington, son Richard and dog, Sire, 1952. (Courtesy of Bill Covington)

Keeper Archie Cameron, Assistant Bob Prueitt, 1952 (top left); Assistant Keeper Gordon Farley, wife Myrtle and their son, 1954 (middle left); Keeper Bill Covington erects first T.V. antenna at Cape Meares. The reception was non-existent most of the time, 1953 (bottom left); Robert Gedlick served at Cape Meares from 1955 to 1961. He was the last officer in charge of the Lighthouse (top right); David Duncan, Bosun's mate 2nd Class, was the last enlisted man to tend the light at Cape Meares (bottom right)

SAGA OF THE ROAD AND OTHER IMPROVEMENTS

The first wagon access to the site was by the short, steep road up the north side of the Cape from Tillamook Bay. This served the purposes for which it was built and the needs of the keepers to bring in supplies from Tillamook City about every three weeks. But a trip to town left a lot to be desired when emergencies arose that didn't coincide with the tide. The following item appeared in the *Tillamook Headlight:*

May 20, 1890. A good wagon road from this place or Tillamook River to Cape Meares Light House would be of great benefit and convenience to the lighthouse.

Date: 1/30/1891

To: Washington, D.C.

From: Hon. J. M. Dolph M. C.

Subject: Cape Meares, Oregon to Tillamook, Oregon roadway by Short Beach, petition endorsed.

Date: 3/6/1891

To: 13th District Inspector

From: Inspector Rhodes

Subject: Cape Meares, Oregon. Roadway by Short Beach recommended.

The wheels of progress can move exceedingly slow. A county road had been built from Tillamook City to the town of Netarts and Netarts Bay. This was known as Hodgdon Road. A petition, signed by most of the prominent business men of the area, was circulated on November 11, 1892 asking the county to extend this road north along the ocean beach to the line of the government reservation of the Cape Meares Lighthouse. County approval was given on December 20, 1892.

Letters continued to be exchanged between the 13th District Engineers and the Treasury Department for the next year and a half. Finally, the slow wheels of government caught up.

Date: 8/16/1893

To: Treasury Department

From: Secretary of Treasury

Subject: Cape Meares, Oregon. Wagon road hired, labor and open purchase authorized.

Improvements, Additions, Repairs

The next major improvement for the light station was the addition of a heated workroom attached to the base of the tower and the replacement of the slippery wooden steps leading from the edge of the trail down to the narrow ledge where the tower sits. The cast iron replacements were a welcome safety factor.

Date: 11/23/1893

To: Treasury Department

From: Secretary of Treasury

Subject: Cape Meares, Oregon. Building workroom with heating arrangement etc. by hired labor authorized

Date: 8/15/1894

To: 13th District

From: Engineer Post

Subject: Cape Meares, Oregon. Construction of work-room and
   wood shed erection, immediate approval requested.

Date: 9/14/1895

To: 13th District

From: Engineer Post

Subject: Cape Meares, Oregon. Water supply repairs, materials.
   Approval of purchase requested.

Date: 5/11/1895

To: 12th District

From: Engineer Fisk

Subject: Cape Meares, Oregon. Wagon road from Light Station to
   Hodgdon Co. Road. Repairs – estimates – costs.
   Recommendation.

Date: 6/6/1896

To: 13th District

From: Engineer Fisk

Subject: Cape Meares, Oregon. Three furnaces for dwellings.
   Purchase authority requested.

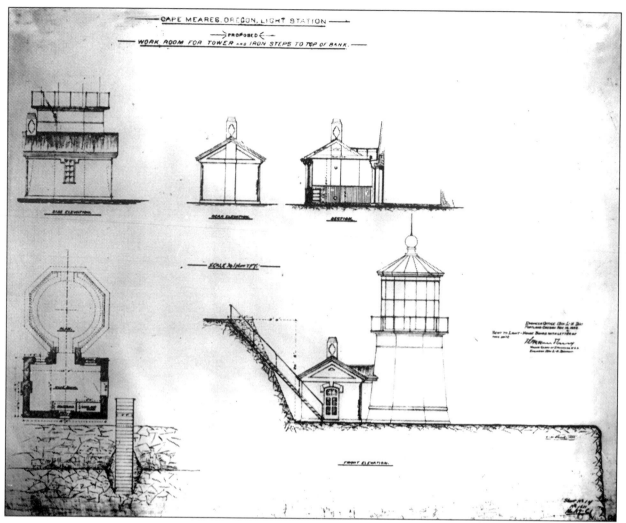

Plans for tower workroom and iron steps—November 16, 1893

Correspondence continued between the 13th District and an assortment of Engineers and Inspectors—most of it relating to personnel. The last letter reference in this fourteen year period follows:

Date: 1/17/1900

To: 13th District

From: Inspector Taussig

Subject: Cape Meares, Oregon Light Station. Second Asst. Keeper
Hermann Grossheim; promotion and transfer to First Asst.
Keeper recommended.

Advances in Lighting Equipment

At Cape Meares the old five-wick lamp was replaced with a new incandescent oil vapor lamp in 1910. In this system kerosene is forced into a hot chamber where it is instantly vaporized when it strikes the hot walls. In this gaseous state, it goes through a series of small holes to a mantle where it burns in a brilliant glowing gas ball.

This is the common system used in contemporary Coleman-type lanterns. Light output from pressurized oil vapor far surpasses any wick-type lamp. The candlepower was significantly increased without using any more oil than the old burners. This was as good as a flame could get.

The next step was electricity. The Lighthouse Board began using it in 1900 and conversions were made when power lines were close to stations. The remote lighthouses had to wait for the installation of generators.

Two Kohler-type engines were installed at Cape Meares in 1934. They supplied enough power for the entire station. One was installed in the base of the tower and the other in the workshop near the houses.

Best of all, when the clockwork that

Automatic light at Cape Meares, 1989.

-View of automatic beacon (the small light) through the old lens opening.

turned the giant lens was electrified, there was no longer a need for hand winding it every two hours. The work of keeping the lens clean was reduced with the elimination of the kerosene lamp. But salt spray was an unending challenge. With electrification the oil storage houses were no longer needed and torn down.

The next step was automation. The new, tiny airways-type beacon light was installed on the end of the cliff behind the tower, about 50 feet east and a bit north of the old sentinel. It is nine feet higher so its beam is not obstructed by the roof of the old tower.

This "mighty mite" produces 2,000,000 candlepower of white light and operates continuously day and night. It was first lit on April 1, 1963. The focal plane was now 232 feet above mean sea level.

National Wildlife Refuge

The 138.51 acres of the Cape Meares Light Station Reserve became Cape Meares Migratory Bird Refuge by Executive Order 7957 dated August 19, 1938 and was signed by President Franklin D. Roosevelt. This was to be a refuge and breeding ground for migratory birds and other wildlife. The name and land status, but not the purpose, was changed to the Cape Meares National Wildlife Refuge by Executive Order 2416 signed July 26, 1940, also by President Roosevelt.

Theodore Roosevelt (1858–1919), President of the United States 1901–1909 (Reproduced from the *Dictionary of American Portraits,* published by Dover Publications, Inc. in 1967)

Franklin Delano Roosevelt (1882–1945), President of the United States 1933–1945 (Reproduced from the *Dictionary of American Portraits,* published by Dover Publications, Inc. in 1967, courtesy Library of Congress)

This new designation did not interfere with the activities of the Lighthouse.

Adjacent to Cape Meares NWR is the Three Arch Rocks National Wildlife Refuge established on October 14, 1907 (with later name changes) by Executive Order 699 signed by President Theodore Roosevelt. This was the first national wildlife refuge west of the Mississippi River. It, along

The Octopus Tree as it appeared in 1964. A fence has since been built to protect the tree.

with Cape Meares and the Oregon Islands NWR (all off-shore islands, rocks and reefs—more than 1,400), have never been in private ownership.

Cape Meares and the Three Arch Rocks were probably used by local native tribes for a variety of purposes. These included fishing, hunting and egg gathering. The over-gathering of eggs by early settlers lead to the Refuge designation. The over two million nesting birds has dwindled to 700,000. But these three National Wildlife Refuges on the Oregon Coast represents 56% of all the known seabirds breeding on the west coast from Mexico to British Columbia.

Seabirds known to breed on Cape Meares are the common murre, tufted puffin, western gull, pelagic cormorant, pigeon guillemot and the black oyster catcher. Peregrine falcons and bald eagles also inhabit the refuge. At least 65 species of seabirds, waterfowl and shorebirds may be seen sometime during the year. Stellar sea lions, California sea lions, harbor seals and an occasional fur seal use the rocks at the base of the Cape and at Three Arch Rocks on their migrations—some are year-around residents. The view from the Lighthouse is outstanding for spotting migrating gray whales and orcas are occasionally seen.

The temperate marine climate is subject to strong winds and tides, especially during winter storms. Gales in excess of 100 miles per hour happen yearly. Temperatures seldom fall to freezing and rarely exceed 75°F. Regular moisture occurs from rain and fog throughout the year, with

The Big Spruce and author to give a sense of scale, 1989.

heavier amounts in the winter. Annual precipitation is around 100 inches.

There is lush temperate rain forest type vegetation. Native Sitka spruce and western hemlock trees with salal and sword fern in the understory are the predominate plants. The average age of trees in the old-growth forest are about 250 years old, with a high percentage of blowdown on the exposed Cape. The down and dead woody debris provides nutrients and seed beds for the next generation. There are two notable exceptions to the age and size of the average tree in the State Park. They are the Octopus Tree and the Big Spruce.

The Octopus Tree is an unusually large Sitka spruce. At its base the diameter is more than ten feet. It has no central trunk, instead several limbs, three to five feet thick, branch out close to the ground before turning up. This accounts for its colorful name. The gale force winds that

buffet its southwestern exposure are probably responsible for its shape. The center trunk was most likely broken off at an early age and its low growing limbs then developed into the present form. The process continues. One huge limb was split and broken during a storm in the winter of 1987–88. There is a legend that claims the tree was altered by the natives for use as a burial tree to hold the canoes of their deceased leaders. There is no documentation of this story. Its isolated location is far from any known Indian village.

The trail to the Big Spruce winds through the forest and the hiker is surprised when the immense tree comes into view. The top of the tree was wind-pruned centuries ago and is now lost in the multiple trunks growing up from branches of the 93 foot crown spread 100 feet above the ground. The trunk is 39 ft. 5 in. in circumference. The diameter is 12 ft. 7 in. The 193 foot tall Sitka spruce is thought to be in excess of 400 years old and is near the largest of its species known. This tree is nature's sentinel on the Cape.

After a noon luncheon in Tillamook, invited guests of the county formed a caravan of cars and headed west. They split into two groups after crossing the Tillamook River. One group traveled on to Netarts then north to Oceanside and on to Cape Meares. The other group drove northwest along the Bayocean Road (finished in 1928) that borders the southern shores of Tillamook Bay and then turns south for a steep climb up to Cape Meares. The meeting of these two groups marked the formal opening of the new county road on October 17, 1960. The same trip by either route now takes less than 20 minutes. This is quite an improvement over what used to take all day.

The new road finally made the lighthouse more accessible to everyone. Turning the site into a State Park now became a feasible possibility. Nine years later the county road was completed to form a loop. This last section, along Netarts Bay and

Formal opening of the loop road from Netarts to the village of Cape Meares, October 17, 1960.

A caravan of cars on their way to the dedication ceremonies.

over the top of Cape Lookout, provided the last link of the Three Capes Scenic Drive. The road links Cape Kiwanda, Cape Lookout and Cape Meares in one of the least seen and most beautiful sections of the Oregon coast.

Decommissioning the Lighthouse

With the coming of the automatic light in 1963, a manned station was no longer necessary. The houses were declared surplus property and were rented by the U.S. Government for several years. The workroom, which was added to the tower in 1894, was removed in 1960. Records have not been located to explain why but vandalism was probably the reason.

County residents became alarmed and were afraid the sturdy little tower was also going to be razed. Public concern led the county to make a lease arrangement with the U.S. Coast Guard on October 23, 1964. The tower is to be used for historic purposes. The abandoned Cape Meares lighthouse was saved from destruction.

Tillamook County Commissioners A.H. Tilden, L.C. Schulmerich and H. Clay Meyers accept the lease for the lighthouse from Coast Guard Keeper Andreasen, Coast Guard Auxiliary Officer Don Benskin and an unidentified member of C.G. Auxiliary Flotilla #64 on November 6, 1964. (Burford Wilkerson Photo, Tillamook, Oregon)

February 14, 1965—Weather observer Don Benskin, Cape Meares Coast Guard Auxiliary, receives a maximum-minimum recording thermometer from L.E. (Stub) Andrus of the Chamber of Commerce Ad Club to help the current fund raising drive for Cape Meares weather station equipment. This station regularly reported to Channel 8 KGW TV weatherman Jack Capel. (Photo by B. Wilkerson, courtesy of Joyce Benskin)

CAPE MEARES STATE SCENIC VIEWPOINT

Further negotiations between Tillamook County and Oregon State Parks led to the county dropping its lease and the Parks signing a new one with the Coast Guard on July 2, 1968. Cape Meares State Park was developed and is managed in conjunction with the Cape Meares National Wildlife Refuge under the U.S. Fish and Wildlife Service. Restroom facilities were completed on November 21, 1975. The reconstruction of the tower workroom was finished and the lighthouse was opened for tours on April 22, 1980. Volunteer "Keepers" host tours of the tower from April through October. The park is primarily a day use area with hiking trails and viewpoints that offer spectacular vistas. Gray whales are often seen from the Cape during their twice-yearly migrations. An increase in visitors now being observed may lead to year-round tours. Cape Lookout State Park, with a full range of overnight camping facilities, is a short drive south.

Near the end of the cape there is an atmospheric sampling station that is directed by the Oregon Graduate Institute of Beaverton, Oregon. This facility monitors air samples hourly for carbon dioxides, carbon monoxides, methane, nitrous oxides, water vapor and chlorofluorocarbons. The Oregon Graduate Institute also operates a station on the South Pacific island of American Samoa. There are other stations on Tasmania, Barbados, Ireland, Point Barrow, Alaska and on Antarctica. The data collected from these seven stations is providing atmospheric scientists with the world-wide information they need to monitor the ozone layer and the heat-trapping greenhouse gases that are influencing global warming. This station has been in operation since May 15, 1978.

In 1988 the U.S. Navy erected a 50 foot pole and instrument box for the installation of a hyper-fix navigation system which is a more sophisticated type of Loran for their

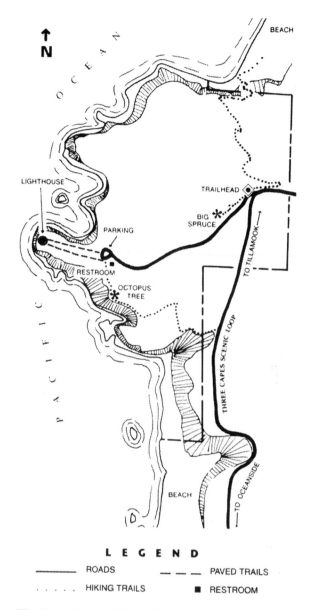

The boundaries of the park also encompass the 138 acre Cape Meares National Wildlife Refuge.

use. This is located on the site of one of the old oil storage buildings where several of the station-made bricks used for their construction were recovered and are now in the collection of the Pioneer Museum. The Friends of Cape Meares is a support group that promotes the preservation of the old Lighthouse, its pristine surroundings and the educational and interpretive programs available there. For more information, contact the volunteer Keepers at the Lighthouse or the Oregon State Parks Office at Cape Lookout State Park.

The Cape Through the Years

Clues to the Past

Dating pictures is a good exercise in observation. Many that appear in the book had no dates at all. Occasionally one would be dated and this would then become a standard by which to compare others. Close attention was given to the type of stairs and railings—we know when these changed.

We watched for changes in the chimney caps and their guy wires. The addition of the water line from the edge of cliff, over the roof of the workroom and ending on the deck of the tower in a water tap was a great clue. The door on the workroom was changed several times. The brickwork of the chimney sometimes was painted with a white center—usually it was all the same color. A wide black band was painted just under the deck from time to time. The growth state of vegetation was another indicator.

One of the most interesting was the change in visitors clothing, especially the ladies and children. Facial hair and hat styles became a tip for men. The oil storage houses were removed in 1934. The garden plot was a sign—little used after transportation improved. Automobiles appeared. The tower workroom was removed in 1960. Then the automatic light building appeared and the dwellings and other outbuildings were removed. Some late photos show damage to the lens.

The air sampling building and new 50 ft. signal pole are later markers. Wildlife information signs were installed in 1995. The Interpretive Kiosk was also built in 1995. Dedication of the signs and kiosk was June 3, 1995. With these clues to guide you, look close and enjoy a trip through time.

Were these early day whale watchers? Circa 1908.

Facing page: Keeper George Hunt on landing and 2nd Assistant Keeper Edward Brooks, watch unidentified workman as he finishes work on the roof of the new workroom in 1895.

View of new workroom and stairs, 1895. Print was made from 5x7 glass plate negative in the Museum's collections.

Keepers quarters at Cape Meares Light Station.

Excellent view of the oil houses which were painted brown. Circa 1899.

Circa 1896 visitors are holding their hats on a windy day. Top from left: Mr. Haley (principal of Tillamook school); Marie Tinnerstet; Frank Warren; Amanda Tinnerstet; Lutie Kuntz; Bob Robins; Frank Haley. On the landng are Bessie Wiley and Bertha Lederer.

Keeper George Hunt is second from left. Circa 1900.

Assistant Keeper George Higgins (second from left) and Mrs. Higgins (on the right) are pictured with an unidentified keeper and wife or friend in this circa 1902 photo. Note the water line had not yet been installed.

Keepers houses and workshop. Note picket fence, privey and large wood piles, circa 1905.

This view shows the waterline and tap and the iron steps, circa 1912.

Binoculars enhance the view for a lady wearing a Keepers hat, circa 1906.

Keepers families in front of picket fence, circa 1910.

Unidentified visitor, circa 1910.

Circa 1911.

Top: Thomas R. Monk of Tillamook took this view of the Lightstation from the northernmost promontory of Cape Meares in 1910.
Bottom: Aerial view taken in 1940.

Keepers and their guests. Circa 1914.

29-CAPE MEARS LIGHT HOUSE, OR.
H. R. GREGG. PHOTO. BAY CITY, ORE.

Left: A keeper is host to visitors, 1913. Above: Fresh coat of paint in 1946. Note larger chimney cap. The Keeper is William Frazier.

Barn and dwellings on a cool day in 1925. The picket fence has been replaced with wire.

Another chore for keepers was maintaining a supply of wood for heating the workroom, circa 1930. Note step ladder next to lens.

Cape Meares — Oregon coast

Cape is clear of vegetation in this early 1930's view.

(Above) Water line has been removed, new stair railing and different door, circa late 1930's. (Right) Storage and power building with oil tank on right, late 1940's.

Unusual light snowfall at the station, 1947.

(Above) Ventilator ball still intact. Different chimney cap, 1949. (Right) View of lighthouse, 1953.

(Top left) In 1968 young visitors can reach the outside landing but the ladder to the deck has been removed. Canvas curtains are still intact. (Top right) Cape Meares Lighthouse, 1980's. (Bottom) Blueprints for new workroom, October 14, 1977

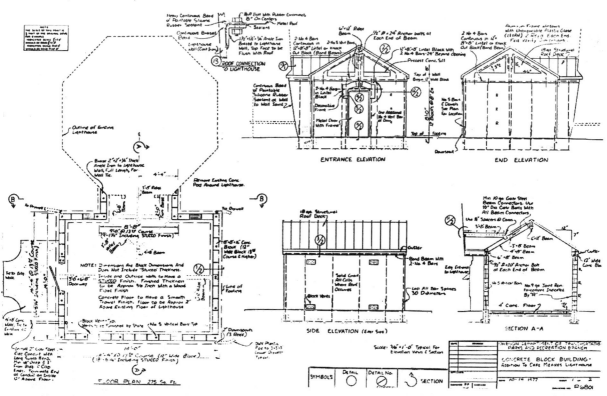

Opposite: (Top) Through the lens, July 1961. (Bottom left) Keeper David Duncan took this view of visitors in 1962. (Bottom right) Workroom was removed in 1960 to discourage vandalism.

Overleaf: Overview—Foreground, north part of Cape Meares, next is the half-mile long finger with Lightstation, Short beach, Maxwell Mountain and Maxwell Point with the largest of the Three Arch Rocks to the right, following is Netarts Bay and sandspit, Cape Lookout extends beyond the edge of the picture, behind it in the far distance is Cascade Head. In the upper left distance is Mt. Hebo. Photo taken in 1963. (Photo by Carl Schonbrod, Tillamook, Oregon)

Other Oregon Lighthouses

Cape Disappointment Lighthouse—1856

The first lighthouse authorized to be built on the west coast in 1849 was at the north entrance to the mouth of the Columbia River in the Oregon Territory. Site preparations were started early in 1853 and the wait for supplies began. The bark *Oriole* had been servicing lighthouse construction sites in California and was finally dispatched to the Columbia. After waiting nine days off the bar the pilot finally took her in on September 19, 1853. The wind died going over the bar and she drifted aground and sank with a complete

Cape Disappointment Lighthouse, circa 1898. Cannons were installed during the Civil War. (Columbia River Maritime Museum, Astoria, Oregon)

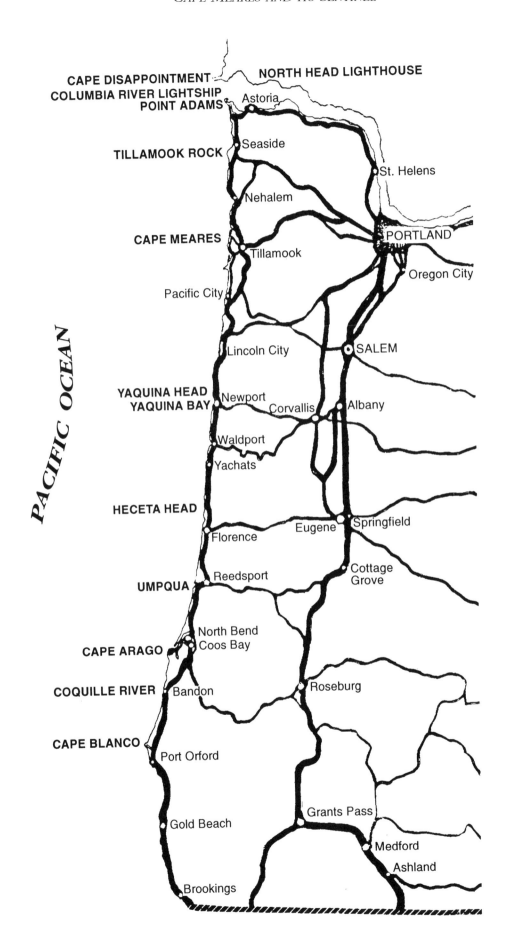

CAPE DISAPPOINTMENT
COLUMBIA RIVER LIGHTSHIP
POINT ADAMS

NORTH HEAD LIGHTHOUSE

Astoria

TILLAMOOK ROCK

Seaside

St. Helens

Nehalem

CAPE MEARES

Tillamook

PORTLAND

Oregon City

Pacific City

Lincoln City

SALEM

YAQUINA HEAD
YAQUINA BAY

Newport

Corvallis

Albany

Waldport

Yachats

HECETA HEAD

Florence

Eugene   Springfield

Reedsport

Cottage
Grove

UMPQUA

North Bend
Coos Bay

CAPE ARAGO

COQUILLE RIVER

Bandon

Roseburg

CAPE BLANCO

Port Orford

Grants Pass

Gold Beach

Medford

Ashland

Brookings

PACIFIC OCEAN

loss of cargo—in sight of and two miles south of Cape Disappointment. The crew was rescued. This disaster further pointed out the need for this desperately needed light at the bar known worldwide as the "Graveyard of Ships."

It was the following year before another supply ship arrived safely. The tower was finished—two more years would pass before there would be a light. Of the first eight lanterns ordered for the Pacific coast, only two could be used without remodeling or rebuilding the towers. The light was finally lit on October 15, 1856. The first order lens was removed to the nearby North Head Lighthouse in 1898. It was replaced by a fourth order lens. The station was fortified during the Civil War with cannons and known as Fort Canby.

The lens was retired from use in the North Head Lighthouse in 1938, and is now on display in the Fort Columbia Historical Society Museum near Chinook, Washington. The tower is 53 feet high, focal plane elevation 220 feet, and visibility 20 miles. It is now automated.

North Head Lighthouse

Columbia Lightship (diesel), WLV 604 on station. (U.S. Coast Guard)

Columbia River Lightship—1892–1979

April 11, 1892 saw *LV 50* (*No. 50*) stationed off the Columbia River entrance 4.4 miles—232° from Cape Disappointment Light but soon moved three miles southwesterly. It was a leading mark for making the approach to the main channel entrance.

This was the first lightship station on the Pacific coast and the last west coast lightship station to be discontinued. Lightships marking the station were blown or dragged off station six times in severe weather. *LV 50* was blown off twice—on November 29, 1899 going aground a quarter-mile mile east of Cape Disappointment. She remained stranded for 16 months before being hauled 700 yards overland and relaunched in Bakers Bay.

After repairs were made she returned to station on May 26, 1902. It happened again on October 6, 1905—she returned to station on October 9, 1906, and served until 1909. Over three years of temporary duty was filled by *LV 67* when filling in for *LV 50*. The next ship assigned was *LV 88/WAL 513* (*No. 88*) in 1909 and she served at that station until 1939.

After a severe storm on November 28–29, 1899, **No. 50,** *the first Columbia River Lightship, having only sails and no power, was blown off station and stranded on the sand inside McKenzie Head. She was jacked up, put on skids and teams of plow horses turned the windlasses to move the ship over a half-mile through timber and several low hills to Bakers Bay. The journey took 16 months. She served until 1909. (U.S. Coast Guard)*

The report of a storm on January 2, 1914, follows "...after steaming ahead for 11 hours, a boarding sea stove in the pilot house, sheared off the steering compass, bent the steering wheel shaft and carried away the bridge binnacle. Also carried away ventilator and galley stack; damaged engine room skylight and flooded engine room; smashed ports in after house and carried away deck stanchions; two crewmen injured by flying glass."

LV 93/WAL 517 (No. 93) served from 1939 to 1951. She survived three memorable storms. *WLV 604* served from 1951 until 1979. She was blown off station during the Columbus Day storm of 1962. The station was discontinued and replaced by Lighted Horn Buoy "CR" (LND). *WLV 604* was decommissioned on December 13, 1979, and sold to the Columbia River Maritime Museum in Astoria, Oregon, where she is now on exhibit. The ships were painted red with COLUMBIA in white. Over the years the position of the ship was changed three times—all within a small range to keep in line with the main river channel. A radio beacon was installed in 1924.

A keeper scans the horizon from atop the Point Adams Lighthouse. (Columbia River Maritime Museum, Astoria, Oregon)

Focal plane elevation varied from 50 feet to 63 feet, visibility varied from 11 miles to 14 miles—a high intensity 600,000 cp light shown from 1960–1979—nominal range 24 miles.

Point Adams—1875–1899

Built at the south entrance to the Columbia River, the lighthouse housed a fourth order lens in a large frame structure. It was situated on a 40 acre plot of the Fort Stevens Military Reservation near Battery Russell in 1875. It displayed a flashing red light that was later changed to fixed red. A red glass chimney was used to produce the color. Several factors were involved in the decision to decommission the light: the stationing of the Columbia River Lightship in 1892; the building of the south jetty which piled tons of material in front of the lighthouse; the construction of the more strategically placed North Head Lighthouse in 1898.

Tillamook Rock Lighthouse

In fact the lightstation was considered a hazard. It was decommissioned on January 31, 1899. The abandoned building was finally burned down on January 12, 1912 by order of the U.S. Secretary of War after several children had been injured while playing in the old structure. The tower was 50 feet high, focal plane elevation 99 feet, visibility 11.1 miles.

Tillamook Rock Lighthouse—1881–1957

A crag of basalt 1.2 miles off Tillamook Head, 20 miles south of the Columbia River, is the site of Tillamook Rock Lighthouse. Access to the rock is one of the most difficult in the world. "Terrible Tilly" made everything difficult—the drenched workmen blasted 29 feet off the top to make a flat surface for the foundation. They had to hammer in ringbolts for handholds while working. Before a derrick could be constructed an engineer was swept to his death while trying to land. Breeches buoy, basket or cargo nets attached by cable to the end of the boom was the only way personnel or supplies could gain access. Even the smallest of craft cannot land under any weather conditions. The building stone for the station was quarried from Mt. Tabor in Portland. Started in the summer of 1870 the first order light was finally lit on January 21, 1881. The storms

Early photo of Yaquina Head Lighthouse. Note barn, fenced pasture and horse. Built in 1874 and still in operation and automated. (Lincoln County Historical Society)

that have raged over the Rock are legendary—with walls of green water and rocks washing completely over the tower and crushing roofs and glass. In 1894 thirteen panels of the lens were smashed. Lens damage happened all too frequently.

Keepers were isolated to the point of starvation on several occasions when seas kept the tenders at bay. Modern navigational aids now keep ships well out to sea and the most costly station ever to maintain was decommissioned on September 1, 1957. The lighthouse was sold in 1973 and again in 1978. After the loss of another life when trying to land a small motorboat, it was sold to its present owners who have turned it into a columbarium—a resting place for the ashes of the dead. Access is now made by helicopter—weather permitting. Focal plane elevation was 133 feet, visibility 20 miles.

Yaquina Head Lighthouse—1873

This lighthouse was built on a headland three and one-half miles north of the Yaquina Bay Lighthouse, 81 feet above the sea. Crews had difficulty landing materials in the small cove below the building site, especially in bad weather—two lighters were lost

Keeper and family at Yaquina Bay Lighthouse, circa 1872. Built in 1871 and discontinued in 1874. (Lincoln County Historical Society)

and the lens was damaged. Confusion was raised over the name of the site. It was called Otter Rock (which is three miles north) by some and Cape Foulweather (which is about seven miles north) by others. Turn of the century photographs often confuse the names. The headland behind the lighthouse has all but disappeared—the basalt making fine road-building materials. The marine gardens at the foot of the headland are now a State Park and a delight to students and visitors at low tide. Permits are required for collecting. The light has been automated in the beautiful old brick and iron tower which is 93 feet high, focal plane elevation 162 feet, visibility 19 miles.

Yaquina Bay Lightouse —1871–1874

For three years this lighthouse provided the guiding light for ships entering Yaquina Bay. It was built on a bluff 100 feet above the north entrance and was intended to be an aid to harbor navigation rather than a coastal light. It was of frame construction with an iron tower to house the lantern. It became

The keepers house was quite a distance away at the Heceta Head Lighthouse. (Columbia River Maritime Museum, Astoria, Oregon)

obsolete and was decommissioned after construction of the first order lighthouse at Yaquina Head in 1873.

The site was deeded to the State of Oregon in 1934 and became a State Park. The structure has been restored and is open for tours. Focal plane elevation was 120 feet.

Heceta Head Lighthouse—1894

The lighthouse, built on one of the most picturesque headlands in the state, was named for Bruno Heceta, an early Spanish explorer. Situated seven and one-half miles north of Florence at the mouth of the Siuslaw River, it perches above the pounding Pacific surf. The entrance to a vast sea lion rookery, one of the largest sea caves in the world, is at the foot of the next headland one mile south of the station. Heceta Head Lighthouse fills a 90-mile gap between Yaquina Head and Cape Arago and its first order lens was a welcome sight to mariners when it was first lit on March 30, 1894. Since the light was automated, the Keepers quarters have been sold

Umpqua River Lighthouse

and are now used for educational conferences and retreats. The area is protected by a State Park. The tower is 56 feet high, focal plane elevation is 205 feet, visibility 21 miles.

Umpqua River Lighthouse—1857

Six sailing vessels were wrecked at the mouth of the Umpqua between 1850 and 1855. The lumber from this port was sorely needed in California and public pressure pushed for the construction of a lighthouse. Theft of supplies and intimidation of the work crews by the local Indians complicated building schedules as did the rainy winter weather. The light was lit in late winter 1857. Built

Cape Arago, U.S. Coast Guard

on the riverbank, the foundation was undermined during a heavy flood and toppled into the river on February 8, 1861. After the mishap, a second-class can buoy was the only navigational aid at the treacherous river entrance for 34 years. The new station was built in 1889 high above the south side of the river in a more practical, protected and beautiful setting. The lamp is automated and the station is now the outstanding feature of Umpqua Lighthouse State Park, Douglas County. The tower is 65 feet high, focal plane elevation 220 feet, visibility 20 miles.

Cape Arago Lighthouse—1866

Erosion has always been a challenge at this site. The first of three lighthouses was erected on a small islet two and one-half miles north of Cape Arago. This geographical feature has had its name Anglicized and was called Cape Gregory. This was the name used when the lighthouse was first commissioned. The U.S. Coast Survey restored the original name a short time later. The lens was transferred from the first truncated-iron structure to a new site on another islet when the wind and waves undermined the first site.

The early keepers also maintained a lifeboat station—the ringing of a large bell would summon nearby volunteers who would rush to

Cape Arago's first lirst lighthouse, circa 1866.

the waiting boats and be off to rig a breeches buoy or pick up survivors from the pounding surf.

In 1934 the station moved again 900 feet south of the first site where a 40 foot high concrete tower was built on a larger islet. It is connected to the mainland by a footbridge. All the latest navigational aids have been concentrated into a very efficient station that serves the Port of Coos Bay—which was one of the largest lumber shipping centers in the world. The now-automated lighthouse is a featured attraction of Cape Arago State Park. Focal plane elevation 100 feet, visibility 22 miles.

Early photo of Coquille River Lightstation. Note elevated walkway from lighthouse to keepers quarters. (Bandon Historical Society, Bandon, Oregon)

Coquille River Lighthouse —1895–1939

Coquille River Lighthouse in Bullards Beach State Park was decommissioned in 1939. The restored structure functions only as a day marker for ships entering the river. An automatic light on the south jetty and a well-buoyed channel have replaced the old "Bandon Light", as it was once known, on the light list.

The masonry conical tower which held a fixed fourth order light and attached fog signal building were one-tenth of a mile away from the frame construction double keepers quarters and barn. They were connected by an elevated wooden walkway. These wooden structures are all gone.

The picturesque lighthouse was restored in 1979, and is now a favorite State Park with both amateur and professional artists and photographers. Focal plane elevation 47 feet, visibility 12 miles.

Cape Blanco, U.S. Coast Guard

Cape Blanco Lighthouse—1870

Oregon's most westerly lighthouse is built on the headland named Cape Blanco by Spanish explorer Martin D'Aguilar in 1603. After engineers rejected two poor shipments of brick, a kiln was built and bricks were made at the site.

Though heavily timbered at the time of construction, the trees were removed from the remote and isolated station for fire safety. The name of the headland had been changed to Cape "Orford" when the lighthouse was built, but by 1889 the name reverted back to the more familiar Cape Blanco.

The waters around the cape are some of the most treacherous on the west coast and even after the lighthouse was built, many ships have been wrecked during the fierce storms that hit the rugged rocky

point. One of the strongest radio beacons on the Pacific coast has
been placed at this station.

The beautiful wildflowers that now cover the cape compete with
the lighthouse for attention at Cape Blanco State Park. The first order
light was first lit on December 20, 1870, and though now automated,
it is the state's oldest continuously operating light. The tower is 59 feet
high, focal plane elevation 245 feet, visibility 26 miles.

BIBLIOGRAPHY

Books

Baldwin, Ewart M. *Geology of Oregon.* University of Oregon, 1964.

Gibbs, James A., Jr. *Sentinels of the North Pacific.* Binford & Mort, 1955.

Holland, Francis R., Jr. *America's Lighthouses.* Stephen Green Press, 1972.

Meares, John *The Memorial of Lt. John Meares.* Ye Galleon Press, 1985.

A Compilation of the Messages and Papers of the Presidents. U.S. Bureau of Literature and Art, 1910.

Wright, E.W. *Lewis & Dryden's Marine History of the Pacific Northwest.* 1895.

Periodicals

Magnum, Doris *Geology of Cape Lookout State Park Near Tillamook, Oregon.* State Dept. of Geology and Mineral Industries, May 1967.

Oregon Historical Society *Oregon Historical Quarterly.* Vol. 2, 14, 27, 35, 38, 51.

U.S. Lighthouse Society *The Keepers Log.* Vol. 11, 1987; Vol. 4, 1989.

Government Periodicals & Documents

U.S. Dept. of Commerce *Lighthouse Service Bulletin.* Vol. V June 1936, Vol. V March 1937, Vol. V May 1939, Vol. V June 1939.

U.S. Treasury Dept. *Coast Guard Bulletin.* Vol. 1, July 1939.

Senate S. 1216 49th Congress 1st Session Jan. 25, 1886.

House H.R. 5862 49th Congress 1st Session June 9, 1886.

National Archives and Records Administration, Washington D.C.— Survey Reports, Maps, Building Plans and Lighthouse Board Letter Indexes.

Newspapers

"Barnegat Post Office Moved to Lighthouse", *Tillamook Headlight,* September 13, 1900.

"Death of Captain George W. Boyington", *Tillamook Headlight,* December 13, 1900.

"Captain George Hunt Married", *Tillamook Headlight,* March 12, 1903.

George Higgins Appointed Assistant Postmaster, *Tillamook Headlight,* May 12, 1903.

"Death of Captain George Hunt", *Tillamook Headlight,* July 16, 1903.

"Captain Charles Miller of Lighthouse in Tillamook", *Tillamook Headlight,* November 11, 1915.

"Captain Charles Miller of Lighthouse in Tillamook", *Tillamook Headlight,* August 17, 1916.

"Lighthouse Road Surveyed", *Tillamook Headlight,* September 4, 1919.

"Captain Andrew Hold, Former Keeper at Cape, Retires", *Tillamook Headlight,* August 21, 1921.

"Cape Meares Lighthouse Being Improved", *Tillamook Headlight,* June 22, 1923.

"Changes at Cape Meares Lighthouse, Keeper Gus Jansen Retires, Charles Miller New Keeper", *Tillamook Headlight,* October 7, 1932.

"Captain Charles Miller Retires from Lighthouse at Cape Meares", *Tillamook Headlight-Herald,* August 17, 1939.

"Gus Jansen Retired Lighthouse Keeper Dies", *Tillamook Headlight-Herald,* March 14, 1940.

"The Misplaced Light House", *Sunday Oregonian* Northwest Magazine, September 12, 1958.

"See Cape Meares Lighthouse", *Tillamook Headlight-Herald,* March 14, 1958.

"Ceremony to Open Cape Meares Drive Along Scenic Coast", *Sunday Oregonian,* October 12, 1960.

"Winds Top 110 Miles on Coast", *Oregonian,* October 12, 1962.

"Lighthouse Will Bow to Automation", *Salem Statesman,* March 10, 1963.

"Historic Lighthouse End Long Tenure", *Tillamook Headlight-Herald,* April 21, 1963.

"Octopus Tree Phenomenon Attracts Much Interest", *Tillamook Headlight-Herald,* May 20, 1963.

"Fate of Famed Cape Meares Lighthouse is in Balance", *Tillamook Headlight-Herald,* August 23, 1964.

"Lighthouse Wins a Stay", *Tillamook Headlight-Herald,* September 19, 1964.

"Approve Tillamook Weather Station", *Tillamook Headlight-Herald,* February 14, 1965.

Acknowledgements

The photo collections and archives of the Tillamook County Pioneer Museum are the framework around which this project was formed. Every undertaking of this kind requires a prodigious amount of research—checking and double-checking. Gaps in the narrative have to be filled—photos of Keepers long since gone are tracked down. Without the generous help of the following people, we would still be searching.

The **Mahler sisters**, **Margaret White** of Newport, Oregon and **Frances LePoividen** of Mesa, Arizona, shared cherished family photos and experiences with us. Other Keepers, families and friends also shared. The list is long. **Barbara Bennett** of Tillamook, Oregon, **Joyce Benskin** of Salem, Oregon, **Floyd Bunn** of Salem, Oregon, **Bill and Virginia Covington** of Bothell, Washington, **Bob Davis** of Bellevue, Washington, **David Duncan** of Dallas, Oregon, **Colleen Fosbind** of Tillamook, Oregon, **Bill Frazier** of Anderson Island, Washington, **Robert Gedlick** of Cove, Oregon, **George Higgins** of Newport, Oregon, **John Horne** of Hayward, California, **Gerry Hysmith** of Tillamook, Oregon, **Jim Mohan,** Oregon Graduate Institute, **Mr. & Mrs. Albert Jansen,** Amity, Oregon, **Carl Schonbrod** of Tillamook, Oregon, **D.H. Shearer** of Tillamook, Oregon, **G.V. Fairfield** of Tillamook, Oregon, **C.F. Stranahan** of Tillamook, Oregon, and **Burford Wilkerson** of Forest Grove, Oregon.

The personnel of the **Oregon State Parks**, particularly **Sallie Jacobson, Pete Marvin, Monte Turner** and **David Talbot. Roy Lowe** of U.S. Fish and Wildlife Service. **Senator Mark O. Hatfield.** Personnel at **Tillamook Bay Coast Guard Station**.

A special appreciation to our sister historical institutions, **Bandon Historical Society** of Bandon, Oregon, **Columbia River Maritime Museum,** Astoria, Oregon, **Lincoln County Historical Society,** Newport, Oregon, **Oregon Historical Society,** Portland, Oregon, **Shore Village Museum,** Rockland, Maine, **Sitka Historical Society,** Sitka, Alaska, **U.S. Lighthouse Society,** San Francisco, California, and an extra special thanks to the **Tillamook County Pioneer Association**.

There is no way to adequately express our gratitude to our dedicated volunteers for the patient hours of proofreading and suggestions they gave—thank you **Kathryn Madsen**, **Helen Schelling** and **Maudie Eastwood**. Thanks to **Linda Gabriel** of the museum staff for the attention she gave to typing and proofing the original manuscript. Thanks to **Ruby Fry-Matson** of the museum staff and especially **Bryce Stetler** for bringing me into the computer age.

C.M. Fairfield
M.W. Jensen, Jr.